TO

FROM

A Creative, Intimate Way
to Grow Closer to God

JOURNALING THROUGH

the Psalms

CHRISTIAN STANDARD BIBLE®

a division of Baker Publishing Group
Minneapolis, Minnesota

© 2017 by Bethany House Publishers

Published by Bethany House Publishers
11400 Hampshire Avenue South
Bloomington, Minnesota 55438
www.bethanyhouse.com

Bethany House Publishers is a division of
Baker Publishing Group, Grand Rapids, Michigan

Printed in China

ISBN: 978-0-7642-1935-1

All rights reserved. No part of this publication may be reproduced, stored in a retrieval system, or transmitted in any form or by any means—for example, electronic, photocopy, recording—without the prior written permission of the publisher. The only exception is brief quotations in printed reviews.

Library of Congress Control Number: 2017933695

All Scripture quotations are taken from the Christian Standard Bible®, Copyright © 2017 by Holman Bible Publishers. Used by permission. Christian Standard Bible® and CSB® are federally registered trademarks of Holman Bible Publishers.

Cover and interior design by Peter Gloege, LOOK Design Studio

Introduction and journal prompts written by Susie Larson

AN INVITATION

I started my morning with joy and expectancy. I hugged my cup of coffee, pored over Scripture, listened to the birds sing, and prayed to a God who is real—who I know hears me when I call on him. The sense of God's presence this morning was absolutely tangible.

But my day turned on a dime when something broke my heart. I looked up and wondered, *How long, Lord? How long until I see you break through in this area of my life? Why do I see so little activity here?*

This is the stuff of life. Lament. Heartbreak. Desperation. Praise. The Psalms reflect the human condition in light of a God who cares, who's involved, and who's still very much at work on the earth today.

Our Savior knows what we need, knows how we need to grow. He knows when learning to trust is better for our souls than getting our way. He speaks and he listens. He guards and he guides. He heals and reveals. He corrects and redirects. And he beautifully breathes life into the very depths of our souls.

The Christian life so often appears to be mostly about outward activity. Yet, at the very center of our lives is a relationship. First and foremost, this faith journey is all about our personal relationship with the One who put the stars in place, who knows our name, who died in our place, who fills us with his Spirit, and who gave us his heaven-breathed Scripture, the precious Word of God.

And at the *center* of his Word we find the Psalms.

Without realizing it, we can too easily approach the Psalms as a spectator, as someone who watches from a distance as the Divine Story plays out before us. But God actually invites us *to participate* with him in the kingdom narrative. His Word is complete—we can add nothing to it nor take anything from it. But his Word is also living, breathing, effective, and powerful, which means that God has something to say to us through his Word today.

Read these psalms, these passionate prayers to the Most High God, and lift your eyes, your voice, and your heart to him. When you speak, he hears you. And he answers. So cry out to him as long as you live.

As you seek shelter under the shadow of his wings, he will cover you with his feathers. His faithful promises will be your armor and protection (Psalm 91:4).

Give yourself some time and space to prayerfully read the Psalms and to prayerfully listen to what the Lord wants to say to you through his inspired Word. He continually leads us to new places of clarity and conviction, purpose and perspective.

> *I will listen to what God will say;*
> *surely the Lord will declare peace*
> *to his people, his godly ones,*
> *and not let them go back to foolish ways.*
>
> PSALM 85:8

Record your insights for future generations so that they may learn from you and more fervently run their own race. You have wisdom, insights, struggles, and triumphs that will mean something to those who come after you. And to journal your journey will do wonders for your own soul. In the days ahead, you'll look back and remember how intimately God has communicated with you. He is with you on this journey.

I pray you'll take time to hear from him each and every day. And may your whole life bear the fruit of your private time spent in that abiding place with our precious Savior.

God is sovereign. Jesus lives. The Spirit breathes. Three in One.

How blessed are we?

May you notice and embrace his presence as you walk this earth. And may your journey through the Psalms draw you into an ever-deepening place of sweetness and dependence upon the One who loves you.

Affectionately his,

Susie Larson

Susie Larson
national speaker, talk radio host,
author of *Your Powerful Prayers*

PSALM 1
The Two Ways

1. How happy is the one who does not
walk in the advice of the wicked
or stand in the pathway with sinners
or sit in the company of mockers!
2. Instead, his delight is in the LORD's instruction,
and he meditates on it day and night.
3. He is like a tree planted beside flowing streams
that bears its fruit in its season
and whose leaf does not wither.
Whatever he does prospers.

4. The wicked are not like this;
instead, they are like chaff that the wind blows away.
5. Therefore the wicked will not stand up in the judgment,
nor sinners in the assembly of the righteous.

6. For the LORD watches over the way of the righteous,
but the way of the wicked leads to ruin.

PSALM 2
Coronation of the Son

1. Why do the nations rage
and the peoples plot in vain?
2. The kings of the earth take their stand,
and the rulers conspire together
against the LORD and his Anointed One:
3. "Let's tear off their chains
and throw their ropes off of us."

4. The one enthroned in heaven laughs;
the Lord ridicules them.
5. Then he speaks to them in his anger
and terrifies them in his wrath:
6. "I have installed my king
on Zion, my holy mountain."

7. I will declare the LORD's decree.
He said to me, "You are my Son;
today I have become your Father.
8. Ask of me,
and I will make the nations your inheritance
and the ends of the earth your possession.
9. You will break them with an iron scepter;
you will shatter them like pottery."

10. So now, kings, be wise;
receive instruction, you judges of the earth.
11. Serve the LORD with reverential awe
and rejoice with trembling.

Consider the streams that flow in and through your life right now. Are they nourishing? Toxic? May Jesus speak to you today.

People and nations often think too highly of themselves and too little of God. What about you? In what ways do you seek his influence?

¹² Pay homage to the Son or he will be angry
and you will perish in your rebellion,
for his anger may ignite at any moment.
All who take refuge in him are happy.

PSALM 3
Confidence in Troubled Times
A psalm of David when he fled from his son Absalom.

¹ LORD, how my foes increase!
There are many who attack me.
² Many say about me,
"There is no help for him in God."   *Selah*

³ But you, LORD, are a shield around me,
my glory, and the one who lifts up my head.
⁴ I cry aloud to the LORD,
and he answers me from his holy mountain.   *Selah*

⁵ I lie down and sleep;
I wake again because the LORD sustains me.
⁶ I will not be afraid of thousands of people
who have taken their stand against me on every side.

⁷ Rise up, LORD!
Save me, my God!
You strike all my enemies on the cheek;
you break the teeth of the wicked.
⁸ Salvation belongs to the LORD;
may your blessing be on your people.   *Selah*

PSALM 4
A Night Prayer
For the choir director: with stringed instruments. A psalm of David.

¹ Answer me when I call,
God, who vindicates me.
You freed me from affliction;
be gracious to me and hear my prayer.

² How long, exalted ones, will my honor be insulted?
How long will you love what is worthless
and pursue a lie?   *Selah*
³ Know that the LORD has set apart
the faithful for himself;
the LORD will hear when I call to him.
⁴ Be angry and do not sin;
on your bed, reflect in your heart and be still.   *Selah*
⁵ Offer sacrifices in righteousness
and trust in the LORD.

⁶ Many are asking, "Who can show us anything good?"
Let the light of your face shine on us, LORD.

In Christ Jesus, favor surrounds you, faith lives in you, and you have a Father who loves you. How is your perspective today? _____

_____
_____
_____
_____
_____
_____
_____

Rehashing offenses holds us captive. Rehearsing his promises sets us free. What is true about you because of Jesus? _____

_____
_____
_____
_____
_____
_____
_____

⁷ You have put more joy in my heart
than they have when their grain and new wine abound.
⁸ I will both lie down and sleep in peace,
for you alone, LORD, make me live in safety.

PSALM 5
The Refuge of the Righteous
For the choir director: with the flutes. A psalm of David.

¹ Listen to my words, LORD;
consider my sighing.
² Pay attention to the sound of my cry,
my King and my God,
for I pray to you.

³ In the morning, LORD, you hear my voice;
in the morning I plead my case to you and watch expectantly.
⁴ For you are not a God who delights in wickedness;
evil cannot dwell with you.
⁵ The boastful cannot stand in your sight;
you hate all evildoers.
⁶ You destroy those who tell lies;
the LORD abhors violent and treacherous people.

⁷ But I enter your house
by the abundance of your faithful love;
I bow down toward your holy temple
in reverential awe of you.
⁸ LORD, lead me in your righteousness
because of my adversaries;
make your way straight before me.

⁹ For there is nothing reliable in what they say;
destruction is within them;
their throat is an open grave;
they flatter with their tongues.
¹⁰ Punish them, God;
let them fall by their own schemes.
Drive them out because of their many crimes,
for they rebel against you.

¹¹ But let all who take refuge in you rejoice;
let them shout for joy forever.
May you shelter them,
and may those who love your name boast about you.
¹² For you, LORD, bless the righteous one;
you surround him with favor like a shield.

Any gift from God's hand pales in comparison to the treasure of knowing his heart. Even so, he invites us to bring our requests to him. Seek his hand and his heart today.

PSALM 6
A Prayer for Mercy

For the choir director: with stringed instruments, according to Sheminith. *A psalm of David.*

1. LORD, do not rebuke me in your anger;
   do not discipline me in your wrath.
2. Be gracious to me, LORD, for I am weak;
   heal me, LORD, for my bones are shaking;
3. my whole being is shaken with terror.
   And you, LORD—how long?

4. Turn, LORD! Rescue me;
   save me because of your faithful love.
5. For there is no remembrance of you in death;
   who can thank you in Sheol?

6. I am weary from my groaning;
   with my tears I dampen my bed
   and drench my couch every night.
7. My eyes are swollen from grief;
   they grow old because of all my enemies.

8. Depart from me, all evildoers,
   for the LORD has heard the sound of my weeping.
9. The LORD has heard my plea for help;
   the LORD accepts my prayer.
10. All my enemies will be ashamed and shake with terror;
    they will turn back and suddenly be disgraced.

PSALM 7
Prayer for Justice

A Shiggaion of David, which he sang to the Lord concerning the words of Cush, a Benjaminite.

1. LORD my God, I seek refuge in you;
   save me from all my pursuers and rescue me
2. or they will tear me like a lion,
   ripping me apart with no one to rescue me.

3. LORD my God, if I have done this,
   if there is injustice on my hands,
4. if I have done harm to one at peace with me
   or have plundered my adversary without cause,
5. may an enemy pursue and overtake me;
   may he trample me to the ground
   and leave my honor in the dust.   Selah

6. Rise up, LORD, in your anger;
   lift yourself up against the fury of my adversaries;
   awake for me;
   you have ordained a judgment.
7. Let the assembly of peoples gather around you;
   take your seat on high over it.

God rescues and redeems. He hears our cries and saves us. How do you need him to intervene? _____

_____
_____
_____
_____
_____
_____
_____

God sees the wicked and cares deeply about the vulnerable. What injustice burdens your heart today? _____

_____
_____
_____
_____
_____
_____
_____

8 The LORD judges the peoples;
  vindicate me, LORD,
  according to my righteousness and my integrity.

9 Let the evil of the wicked come to an end,
  but establish the righteous.
  The one who examines the thoughts and emotions
  is a righteous God.
10 My shield is with God,
  who saves the upright in heart.
11 God is a righteous judge
  and a God who shows his wrath every day.

12 If anyone does not repent,
  he will sharpen his sword;
  he has strung his bow and made it ready.
13 He has prepared his deadly weapons;
  he tips his arrows with fire.

14 See, the wicked one is pregnant with evil,
  conceives trouble, and gives birth to deceit.
15 He dug a pit and hollowed it out
  but fell into the hole he had made.
16 His trouble comes back on his own head;
  his own violence comes down on top of his head.

17 I will thank the LORD for his righteousness;
  I will sing about the name of the LORD Most High.

PSALM 8
God's Glory, Human Dignity
For the choir director: on the Gittith. *A psalm of David.*

1 LORD, our Lord,
  how magnificent is your name throughout the earth!

  You have covered the heavens with your majesty.
2 From the mouths of infants and nursing babies,
  you have established a stronghold
  on account of your adversaries
  in order to silence the enemy and the avenger.

3 When I observe your heavens,
  the work of your fingers,
  the moon and the stars,
  which you set in place,
4 what is a human being that you remember him,
  a son of man that you look after him?
5 You made him little less than God
  and crowned him with glory and honor.
6 You made him ruler over the works of your hands;
  you put everything under his feet:

Whatever you are facing, remember this: God is stronger still. Seek his face and his strength.

⁷ all the sheep and oxen,
   as well as the animals in the wild,
⁸ the birds of the sky,
   and the fish of the sea
   that pass through the currents of the seas.

⁹ LORD, our Lord,
   how magnificent is your name throughout the earth!

PSALM 9
Celebration of God's Justice
*For the choir director: according to Muth-labben.
A psalm of David.*

¹ I will thank the LORD with all my heart;
   I will declare all your wondrous works.
² I will rejoice and boast about you;
   I will sing about your name, Most High.

³ When my enemies retreat,
   they stumble and perish before you.
⁴ For you have upheld my just cause;
   you are seated on your throne as a righteous judge.
⁵ You have rebuked the nations:
   You have destroyed the wicked;
   you have erased their name forever and ever.
⁶ The enemy has come to eternal ruin.
   You have uprooted the cities,
   and the very memory of them has perished.

⁷ But the LORD sits enthroned forever;
   he has established his throne for judgment.
⁸ And he judges the world with righteousness;
   he executes judgment on the nations with fairness.
⁹ The LORD is a refuge for the persecuted,
   a refuge in times of trouble.
¹⁰ Those who know your name trust in you
   because you have not abandoned
   those who seek you, LORD.

¹¹ Sing to the LORD, who dwells in Zion;
   proclaim his deeds among the nations.
¹² For the one who seeks an accounting
   for bloodshed remembers them;
   he does not forget the cry of the oppressed.

¹³ Be gracious to me, LORD;
   consider my affliction at the hands of those who hate me.
   Lift me up from the gates of death,
¹⁴ so that I may declare all your praises.
   I will rejoice in your salvation
   within the gates of Daughter Zion.

Which blessings do you tend to take for granted? Freedom? Food? Fellowship? Thank him today.

¹⁵ The nations have fallen into the pit they made;
   their foot is caught in the net they have concealed.
¹⁶ The LORD has made himself known;
   he has executed justice,
   snaring the wicked
   by the work of their hands. *Higgaion. Selah*

¹⁷ The wicked will return to Sheol—
   all the nations that forget God.
¹⁸ For the needy will not always be forgotten;
   the hope of the oppressed will not perish forever.

¹⁹ Rise up, LORD! Do not let mere humans prevail;
   let the nations be judged in your presence.
²⁰ Put terror in them, LORD;
   let the nations know they are only humans. *Selah*

PSALM 10
Need for God's Justice

¹ LORD, why do you stand so far away?
  Why do you hide in times of trouble?
² In arrogance the wicked relentlessly pursue their victims;
  let them be caught in the schemes they have devised.

³ For the wicked one boasts about his own cravings;
  the one who is greedy curses and despises the LORD.
⁴ In all his scheming,
  the wicked person arrogantly thinks,
  "There's no accountability,
  since there's no God."
⁵ His ways are always secure;
  your lofty judgments have no effect on him;
  he scoffs at all his adversaries.
⁶ He says to himself, "I will never be moved—
  from generation to generation without calamity."
⁷ Cursing, deceit, and violence fill his mouth;
  trouble and malice are under his tongue.
⁸ He waits in ambush near settlements;
  he kills the innocent in secret places.
  His eyes are on the lookout for the helpless;
⁹ he lurks in secret like a lion in a thicket.
  He lurks in order to seize a victim;
  he seizes a victim and drags him in his net.
¹⁰ So he is oppressed and beaten down;
   helpless people fall because of the wicked one's strength.
¹¹ He says to himself, "God has forgotten;
   he hides his face and will never see."

¹² Rise up, LORD God! Lift up your hand.
   Do not forget the oppressed.

Even when it feels like God is absent or when it seems he is uninvolved, remember this: He is near and he cares. He will one day put things right again. Remind your soul what is true.

¹³ Why has the wicked person despised God?
   He says to himself, "You will not demand an account."
¹⁴ But you yourself have seen trouble and grief,
   observing it in order to take the matter into your hands.
   The helpless one entrusts himself to you;
   you are a helper of the fatherless.
¹⁵ Break the arm of the wicked, evil person,
   until you look for his wickedness,
   but it can't be found.

¹⁶ The LORD is King forever and ever;
   the nations will perish from his land.
¹⁷ LORD, you have heard the desire of the humble;
   you will strengthen their hearts.
   You will listen carefully,
¹⁸ doing justice for the fatherless and the oppressed
   so that mere humans from the earth may terrify them no more.

PSALM 11
Refuge in the Lord
For the choir director. Of David.

¹ I have taken refuge in the LORD.
  How can you say to me,
  "Escape to the mountains like a bird!
² For look, the wicked string bows;
  they put their arrows on bowstrings
  to shoot from the shadows at the upright in heart.
³ When the foundations are destroyed,
  what can the righteous do?"

⁴ The LORD is in his holy temple;
  the LORD—his throne is in heaven.
  His eyes watch;
  his gaze examines everyone.
⁵ The LORD examines the righteous,
  but he hates the wicked
  and those who love violence.
⁶ Let him rain burning coals and sulfur on the wicked;
  let a scorching wind be the portion in their cup.
⁷ For the LORD is righteous; he loves righteous deeds.
  The upright will see his face.

We can run away in fear or run to God in faith. What are your fears telling you today? What does God say?

PSALM 12
Oppression by the Wicked
For the choir director: according to Sheminith. *A psalm of David.*

1. Help, LORD, for no faithful one remains;
   the loyal have disappeared from the human race.
2. They lie to one another;
   they speak with flattering lips and deceptive hearts.
3. May the LORD cut off all flattering lips
   and the tongue that speaks boastfully.
4. They say, "Through our tongues we have power;
   our lips are our own—who can be our master?"

5. "Because of the devastation of the needy
   and the groaning of the poor,
   I will now rise up," says the LORD.
   "I will provide safety for the one who longs for it."

6. The words of the LORD are pure words,
   like silver refined in an earthen furnace,
   purified seven times.
7. You, LORD, will guard us;
   you will protect us from this generation forever.
8. The wicked prowl all around,
   and what is worthless is exalted by the human race.

PSALM 13
A Plea for Deliverance
For the choir director. A psalm of David.

1. How long, LORD? Will you forget me forever?
   How long will you hide your face from me?
2. How long will I store up anxious concerns within me,
   agony in my mind every day?
   How long will my enemy dominate me?

3. Consider me and answer, LORD my God.
   Restore brightness to my eyes;
   otherwise, I will sleep in death.
4. My enemy will say, "I have triumphed over him,"
   and my foes will rejoice because I am shaken.

5. But I have trusted in your faithful love;
   my heart will rejoice in your deliverance.
6. I will sing to the LORD
   because he has treated me generously.

How would your neighborhood change if people feared God? How would salvation impact your lost loved ones? Dream a little.

Can you sing in the rain before the answer comes? What blessings can you thank God for today?

PSALM 14
A Portrait of Sinners
For the choir director. Of David.

1. The fool says in his heart, "There's no God."
They are corrupt; they do vile deeds.
There is no one who does good.
2. The LORD looks down from heaven on the human race
to see if there is one who is wise,
one who seeks God.
3. All have turned away;
all alike have become corrupt.
There is no one who does good,
not even one.

4. Will evildoers never understand?
They consume my people as they consume bread;
they do not call on the LORD.

5. Then they will be filled with dread,
for God is with those who are righteous.
6. You sinners frustrate the plans of the oppressed,
but the LORD is his refuge.

7. Oh, that Israel's deliverance would come from Zion!
When the LORD restores the fortunes of his people,
let Jacob rejoice, let Israel be glad.

PSALM 15
A Description of the Godly
A psalm of David.

1. LORD, who can dwell in your tent?
Who can live on your holy mountain?

2. The one who lives blamelessly, practices righteousness,
and acknowledges the truth in his heart—
3. who does not slander with his tongue,
who does not harm his friend
or discredit his neighbor,
4. who despises the one rejected by the LORD
but honors those who fear the LORD,
who keeps his word whatever the cost,
5. who does not lend his silver at interest
or take a bribe against the innocent—
the one who does these things will never be shaken.

Sin pulls us downward, but the Spirit of God within us calls us upward. He often calls us away from one thing to call us toward another. What is he saying to you? _____

_____
_____
_____
_____
_____
_____

Because of Christ we can enter God's presence with holy confidence and humble dependence. Thank God for his indescribable gift!

_____
_____
_____
_____
_____
_____
_____

PSALM 16
Confidence in the Lord
A Miktam of David.

1. Protect me, God, for I take refuge in you.
2. I said to the LORD, "You are my Lord;
   I have nothing good besides you."
3. As for the holy people who are in the land,
   they are the noble ones.
   All my delight is in them.
4. The sorrows of those who take another god
   for themselves will multiply;
   I will not pour out their drink offerings of blood,
   and I will not speak their names with my lips.

5. LORD, you are my portion
   and my cup of blessing;
   you hold my future.
6. The boundary lines have fallen for me
   in pleasant places;
   indeed, I have a beautiful inheritance.

7. I will bless the LORD who counsels me—
   even at night when my thoughts trouble me.
8. I always let the LORD guide me.
   Because he is at my right hand,
   I will not be shaken.

9. Therefore my heart is glad
   and my whole being rejoices;
   my body also rests securely.
10. For you will not abandon me to Sheol;
    you will not allow your faithful one to see decay.
11. You reveal the path of life to me;
    in your presence is abundant joy;
    at your right hand are eternal pleasures.

PSALM 17
A Prayer for Protection
A prayer of David.

1. LORD, hear a just cause;
   pay attention to my cry;
   listen to my prayer—
   from lips free of deceit.
2. Let my vindication come from you,
   for you see what is right.
3. You have tested my heart;
   you have examined me at night.
   You have tried me and found nothing evil;
   I have determined that my mouth will not sin.

Spend time thanking God for your influence, territory, and current assignment. Ask him to help you fill your space and run your race.

⁴ Concerning what people do:
by the words from your lips
I have avoided the ways of the violent.
⁵ My steps are on your paths;
my feet have not slipped.

⁶ I call on you, God,
because you will answer me;
listen closely to me; hear what I say.
⁷ Display the wonders of your faithful love,
Savior of all who seek refuge
from those who rebel against your right hand.
⁸ Protect me as the pupil of your eye;
hide me in the shadow of your wings
⁹ from the wicked who treat me violently,
my deadly enemies who surround me.

¹⁰ They are uncaring;
their mouths speak arrogantly.
¹¹ They advance against me; now they surround me.
They are determined
to throw me to the ground.
¹² They are like a lion eager to tear,
like a young lion lurking in ambush.

¹³ Rise up, LORD!
Confront him; bring him down.
With your sword, save me from the wicked.
¹⁴ With your hand, LORD, save me from men,
from men of the world
whose portion is in this life:
You fill their bellies with what you have in store;
their sons are satisfied,
and they leave their surplus to their children.

¹⁵ But I will see your face in righteousness;
when I awake, I will be satisfied with your presence.

PSALM 18
Praise for Deliverance

For the choir director. Of the servant of the Lord, David, who spoke the words of this song to the Lord on the day the Lord rescued him from the grasp of all his enemies and from the power of Saul. He said:

¹ I love you, LORD, my strength.
² The LORD is my rock,
my fortress, and my deliverer,
my God, my rock where I seek refuge,
my shield and the horn of my salvation,
my stronghold.
³ I called to the LORD, who is worthy of praise,
and I was saved from my enemies.

In every generation, the wicked prosper until God intervenes. Stand in the gap for the vulnerable today. May God bring justice in miraculous ways!

⁴ The ropes of death were wrapped around me;
   the torrents of destruction terrified me.
⁵ The ropes of Sheol entangled me;
   the snares of death confronted me.
⁶ I called to the LORD in my distress,
   and I cried to my God for help.
   From his temple he heard my voice,
   and my cry to him reached his ears.

⁷ Then the earth shook and quaked;
   the foundations of the mountains trembled;
   they shook because he burned with anger.
⁸ Smoke rose from his nostrils,
   and consuming fire came from his mouth;
   coals were set ablaze by it.
⁹ He bent the heavens and came down,
   total darkness beneath his feet.
¹⁰ He rode on a cherub and flew,
   soaring on the wings of the wind.
¹¹ He made darkness his hiding place,
   dark storm clouds his canopy around him.
¹² From the radiance of his presence,
   his clouds swept onward with hail and blazing coals.
¹³ The LORD thundered from heaven;
   the Most High made his voice heard.
¹⁴ He shot his arrows and scattered them;
   he hurled lightning bolts and routed them.
¹⁵ The depths of the sea became visible,
   the foundations of the world were exposed,
   at your rebuke, LORD,
   at the blast of the breath of your nostrils.

¹⁶ He reached down from on high
   and took hold of me;
   he pulled me out of deep water.
¹⁷ He rescued me from my powerful enemy
   and from those who hated me,
   for they were too strong for me.
¹⁸ They confronted me in the day of my calamity,
   but the LORD was my support.
¹⁹ He brought me out to a spacious place;
   he rescued me because he delighted in me.

²⁰ The LORD rewarded me
   according to my righteousness;
   he repaid me
   according to the cleanness of my hands.
²¹ For I have kept the ways of the LORD
   and have not turned from my God to wickedness.
²² Indeed, I let all his ordinances guide me
   and have not disregarded his statutes.

God uses our hardships to train us for battle. He defends and delivers. He redeems and remembers his promises. Call on him today.

²³ I was blameless toward him
and kept myself from my iniquity.
²⁴ So the LORD repaid me
according to my righteousness,
according to the cleanness of my hands in his sight.

²⁵ With the faithful
you prove yourself faithful,
with the blameless
you prove yourself blameless,
²⁶ with the pure
you prove yourself pure;
but with the crooked
you prove yourself shrewd.
²⁷ For you rescue an oppressed people,
but you humble those with haughty eyes.
²⁸ LORD, you light my lamp;
my God illuminates my darkness.
²⁹ With you I can attack a barricade,
and with my God I can leap over a wall.

³⁰ God—his way is perfect;
the word of the LORD is pure.
He is a shield to all who take refuge in him.
³¹ For who is God besides the LORD?
And who is a rock? Only our God.
³² God—he clothes me with strength
and makes my way perfect.
³³ He makes my feet like the feet of a deer
and sets me securely on the heights.
³⁴ He trains my hands for war;
my arms can bend a bow of bronze.
³⁵ You have given me the shield of your salvation;
your right hand upholds me,
and your humility exalts me.
³⁶ You make a spacious place beneath me for my steps,
and my ankles do not give way.
³⁷ I pursue my enemies and overtake them;
I do not turn back until they are wiped out.
³⁸ I crush them, and they cannot get up;
they fall beneath my feet.
³⁹ You have clothed me with strength for battle;
you subdue my adversaries beneath me.
⁴⁰ You have made my enemies retreat before me;
I annihilate those who hate me.
⁴¹ They cry for help, but there is no one to save them—
they cry to the LORD, but he does not answer them.
⁴² I pulverize them like dust before the wind;
I trample them like mud in the streets.

⁴³ You have freed me from the feuds among the people;
  you have appointed me the head of nations;
  a people I had not known serve me.
⁴⁴ Foreigners submit to me cringing;
  as soon as they hear they obey me.
⁴⁵ Foreigners lose heart
  and come trembling from their fortifications.

⁴⁶ The LORD lives—blessed be my rock!
  The God of my salvation is exalted.
⁴⁷ God—he grants me vengeance
  and subdues peoples under me.
⁴⁸ He frees me from my enemies.
  You exalt me above my adversaries;
  you rescue me from violent men.
⁴⁹ Therefore I will give thanks to you among the nations, LORD;
  I will sing praises about your name.
⁵⁰ He gives great victories to his king;
  he shows loyalty to his anointed,
  to David and his descendants forever.

PSALM 19
The Witness of Creation and Scripture
For the choir director. A psalm of David.

¹ The heavens declare the glory of God,
  and the expanse proclaims the work of his hands.
² Day after day they pour out speech;
  night after night they communicate knowledge.
³ There is no speech; there are no words;
  their voice is not heard.
⁴ Their message has gone out to the whole earth,
  and their words to the ends of the world.

  In the heavens he has pitched a tent for the sun.
⁵ It is like a bridegroom coming from his home;
  it rejoices like an athlete running a course.
⁶ It rises from one end of the heavens
  and circles to their other end;
  nothing is hidden from its heat.

⁷ The instruction of the LORD is perfect,
  renewing one's life;
  the testimony of the LORD is trustworthy,
  making the inexperienced wise.
⁸ The precepts of the LORD are right,
  making the heart glad;
  the command of the LORD is radiant,
  making the eyes light up.

Look out the window today and notice the Lord's handiwork. Our star-breathing God speaks truth to your heart. Listen to what he has to say to you.

9 The fear of the LORD is pure,
  enduring forever;
  the ordinances of the LORD are reliable
  and altogether righteous.
10 They are more desirable than gold—
  than an abundance of pure gold;
  and sweeter than honey
  dripping from a honeycomb.
11 In addition, your servant is warned by them,
  and in keeping them there is an abundant reward.

12 Who perceives his unintentional sins?
  Cleanse me from my hidden faults.
13 Moreover, keep your servant from willful sins;
  do not let them rule me.
  Then I will be blameless
  and cleansed from blatant rebellion.
14 May the words of my mouth
  and the meditation of my heart
  be acceptable to you,
  LORD, my rock and my Redeemer.

PSALM 20
Deliverance in Battle
For the choir director. A psalm of David.

1 May the LORD answer you in a day of trouble;
  may the name of Jacob's God protect you.
2 May he send you help from the sanctuary
  and sustain you from Zion.
3 May he remember all your offerings
  and accept your burnt offering.   *Selah*

4 May he give you what your heart desires
  and fulfill your whole purpose.
5 Let us shout for joy at your victory
  and lift the banner in the name of our God.
  May the LORD fulfill all your requests.
6 Now I know that the LORD gives victory to his anointed;
  he will answer him from his holy heaven
  with mighty victories from his right hand.
7 Some take pride in chariots, and others in horses,
  but we take pride in the name of the LORD our God.
8 They collapse and fall,
  but we rise and stand firm.
9 LORD, give victory to the king!
  May he answer us on the day that we call.

When our souls are troubled, it's tempting to grab quick solutions. But our help comes from God. Wait on him today. Entrust your desires to him.

PSALM 21
The King's Victory
For the choir director. A psalm of David.

1 LORD, the king finds joy in your strength.
How greatly he rejoices in your victory!
2 You have given him his heart's desire
and have not denied the request of his lips.   *Selah*
3 For you meet him with rich blessings;
you place a crown of pure gold on his head.
4 He asked you for life, and you gave it to him—
length of days forever and ever.
5 His glory is great through your victory;
you confer majesty and splendor on him.
6 You give him blessings forever;
you cheer him with joy in your presence.
7 For the king relies on the LORD;
through the faithful love of the Most High
he is not shaken.

8 Your hand will capture all your enemies;
your right hand will seize those who hate you.
9 You will make them burn
like a fiery furnace when you appear;
the LORD will engulf them in his wrath,
and fire will devour them.
10 You will wipe their progeny from the earth
and their offspring from the human race.
11 Though they intend to harm you
and devise a wicked plan, they will not prevail.
12 Instead, you will put them to flight
when you ready your bowstrings to shoot at them.

13 Be exalted, LORD, in your strength;
we will sing and praise your might.

PSALM 22
From Suffering to Praise
For the choir director: according to "The Deer of the Dawn." A psalm of David.

1 My God, my God, why have you abandoned me?
Why are you so far from my deliverance
and from my words of groaning?
2 My God, I cry by day, but you do not answer,
by night, yet I have no rest.
3 But you are holy,
enthroned on the praises of Israel.
4 Our fathers trusted in you;
they trusted, and you rescued them.
5 They cried to you and were set free;
they trusted in you and were not disgraced.

Has God restored something you thought you lost? Thank him today! Pray too for the injustices in our culture.

⁶ But I am a worm and not a man,
   scorned by mankind and despised by people.
⁷ Everyone who sees me mocks me;
   they sneer and shake their heads:
⁸ "He relies on the LORD;
   let him save him;
   let the LORD rescue him,
   since he takes pleasure in him."

⁹ It was you who brought me out of the womb,
   making me secure at my mother's breast.
¹⁰ I was given over to you at birth;
    you have been my God from my mother's womb.

¹¹ Don't be far from me, because distress is near
    and there's no one to help.
¹² Many bulls surround me;
    strong ones of Bashan encircle me.
¹³ They open their mouths against me—
    lions, mauling and roaring.
¹⁴ I am poured out like water,
    and all my bones are disjointed;
    my heart is like wax,
    melting within me.
¹⁵ My strength is dried up like baked clay;
    my tongue sticks to the roof of my mouth.
    You put me into the dust of death.
¹⁶ For dogs have surrounded me;
    a gang of evildoers has closed in on me;
    they pierced my hands and my feet.
¹⁷ I can count all my bones;
    people look and stare at me.
¹⁸ They divided my garments among themselves,
    and they cast lots for my clothing.

¹⁹ But you, LORD, don't be far away.
    My strength, come quickly to help me.
²⁰ Rescue my life from the sword,
    my only life from the power of these dogs.
²¹ Save me from the lion's mouth,
    from the horns of wild oxen.

You answered me!
²² I will proclaim your name to my brothers and sisters;
    I will praise you in the assembly.
²³ You who fear the LORD, praise him!
    All you descendants of Jacob, honor him!
    All you descendants of Israel, revere him!
²⁴ For he has not despised or abhorred
    the torment of the oppressed.
    He did not hide his face from him
    but listened when he cried to him for help.

Right here, in the midst of your unanswered prayers, can you declare that God is holy, just, and good? You will persevere! Thank God ahead of time.

²⁵ I will give praise in the great assembly
 because of you;
 I will fulfill my vows
 before those who fear you.
²⁶ The humble will eat and be satisfied;
 those who seek the LORD will praise him.
 May your hearts live forever!
²⁷ All the ends of the earth will remember
 and turn to the LORD.
 All the families of the nations
 will bow down before you,
²⁸ for kingship belongs to the LORD;
 he rules the nations.
²⁹ All who prosper on earth will eat and bow down;
 all those who go down to the dust
 will kneel before him—
 even the one who cannot preserve his life.
³⁰ Their descendants will serve him;
 the next generation will be told about the Lord.
³¹ They will come and declare his righteousness;
 to a people yet to be born
 they will declare what he has done.

PSALM 23
The Good Shepherd
A psalm of David.

¹ The LORD is my shepherd;
 I have what I need.
² He lets me lie down in green pastures;
 he leads me beside quiet waters.
³ He renews my life;
 he leads me along the right paths
 for his name's sake.
⁴ Even when I go through the darkest valley,
 I fear no danger,
 for you are with me;
 your rod and your staff—they comfort me.

⁵ You prepare a table before me
 in the presence of my enemies;
 you anoint my head with oil;
 my cup overflows.
⁶ Only goodness and faithful love will pursue me
 all the days of my life,
 and I will dwell in the house of the LORD
 as long as I live.

In Christ Jesus, you lack no good thing. Need rest? Protection? Direction? Draw near to him today and follow his lead.

PSALM 24
The King of Glory
A psalm of David.

1 The earth and everything in it,
the world and its inhabitants,
belong to the LORD;
2 for he laid its foundation on the seas
and established it on the rivers.

3 Who may ascend the mountain of the LORD?
Who may stand in his holy place?
4 The one who has clean hands and a pure heart,
who has not appealed to what is false,
and who has not sworn deceitfully.
5 He will receive blessing from the LORD,
and righteousness from the God of his salvation.
6 Such is the generation of those who inquire of him,
who seek the face of the God of Jacob. *Selah*

7 Lift up your heads, you gates!
Rise up, ancient doors!
Then the King of glory will come in.
8 Who is this King of glory?
The LORD, strong and mighty,
the LORD, mighty in battle.
9 Lift up your heads, you gates!
Rise up, ancient doors!
Then the King of glory will come in.
10 Who is he, this King of glory?
The LORD of Armies,
he is the King of glory. *Selah*

PSALM 25
Dependence on the Lord
Of David.

1 LORD, I appeal to you.
2 My God, I trust in you.
Do not let me be disgraced;
do not let my enemies gloat over me.
3 No one who waits for you
will be disgraced;
those who act treacherously without cause
will be disgraced.

4 Make your ways known to me, LORD;
teach me your paths.
5 Guide me in your truth and teach me,
for you are the God of my salvation;
I wait for you all day long.

Look around and notice the sky, the birds, and the trees. The Lord made these and he made you, all for his glory. What most distracts you from the glory around and in you? _____

⁶ Remember, LORD, your compassion
   and your faithful love,
   for they have existed from antiquity.
⁷ Do not remember the sins of my youth
   or my acts of rebellion;
   in keeping with your faithful love, remember me
   because of your goodness, LORD.

⁸ The LORD is good and upright;
   therefore he shows sinners the way.
⁹ He leads the humble in what is right
   and teaches them his way.
¹⁰ All the LORD's ways show faithful love and truth
   to those who keep his covenant and decrees.
¹¹ LORD, for the sake of your name,
   forgive my iniquity, for it is immense.

¹² Who is this person who fears the LORD?
   He will show him the way he should choose.
¹³ He will live a good life,
   and his descendants will inherit the land.
¹⁴ The secret counsel of the LORD
   is for those who fear him,
   and he reveals his covenant to them.
¹⁵ My eyes are always on the LORD,
   for he will pull my feet out of the net.

¹⁶ Turn to me and be gracious to me,
   for I am alone and afflicted.
¹⁷ The distresses of my heart increase;
   bring me out of my sufferings.
¹⁸ Consider my affliction and trouble,
   and forgive all my sins.
¹⁹ Consider my enemies; they are numerous,
   and they hate me violently.
²⁰ Guard me and rescue me;
   do not let me be put to shame,
   for I take refuge in you.
²¹ May integrity and what is right
   watch over me,
   for I wait for you.
²² God, redeem Israel, from all its distresses.

PSALM 26
Prayer for Vindication
Of David.

¹ Vindicate me, LORD,
   because I have lived with integrity
   and have trusted in the LORD without wavering.

We are prone to wander in our thoughts, perspective, and even our deeds. How is God calling you back to the path of life? How will you respond?

2 Test me, LORD, and try me;
  examine my heart and mind.
3 For your faithful love guides me,
  and I live by your truth.

4 I do not sit with the worthless
  or associate with hypocrites.
5 I hate a crowd of evildoers,
  and I do not sit with the wicked.
6 I wash my hands in innocence
  and go around your altar, LORD,
7 raising my voice in thanksgiving
  and telling about your wondrous works.

8 LORD, I love the house where you dwell,
  the place where your glory resides.
9 Do not destroy me along with sinners,
  or my life along with men of bloodshed
10 in whose hands are evil schemes
  and whose right hands are filled with bribes.

11 But I live with integrity;
  redeem me and be gracious to me.
12 My foot stands on level ground;
  I will bless the LORD in the assemblies.

PSALM 27
My Stronghold
Of David.

1 The LORD is my light and my salvation—
  whom should I fear?
  The LORD is the stronghold of my life—
  whom should I dread?
2 When evildoers came against me to devour my flesh,
  my foes and my enemies stumbled and fell.
3 Though an army deploys against me,
  my heart will not be afraid;
  though a war breaks out against me,
  I will still be confident.

4 I have asked one thing from the LORD;
  it is what I desire:
  to dwell in the house of the LORD
  all the days of my life,
  gazing on the beauty of the LORD
  and seeking him in his temple.
5 For he will conceal me in his shelter
  in the day of adversity;
  he will hide me under the cover of his tent;
  he will set me high on a rock.

God delivers and defends. In every season he deserves our praise. Tell him what you need and thank him for what he has done. He is profoundly good!

Tune out the noises of the world and bend an ear toward God. Find your confidence in him. What is he saying to you today?

⁶ Then my head will be high
above my enemies around me;
I will offer sacrifices in his tent with shouts of joy.
I will sing and make music to the LORD.

⁷ LORD, hear my voice when I call;
be gracious to me and answer me.
⁸ My heart says this about you:
"Seek his face."
LORD, I will seek your face.
⁹ Do not hide your face from me;
do not turn your servant away in anger.
You have been my helper;
do not leave me or abandon me,
God of my salvation.
¹⁰ Even if my father and mother abandon me,
the LORD cares for me.

¹¹ Because of my adversaries,
show me your way, LORD,
and lead me on a level path.
¹² Do not give me over to the will of my foes,
for false witnesses rise up against me,
breathing violence.

¹³ I am certain that I will see the LORD's goodness
in the land of the living.
¹⁴ Wait for the LORD;
be strong, and let your heart be courageous.
Wait for the LORD.

PSALM 28
My Strength
Of David.

¹ LORD, I call to you;
my rock, do not be deaf to me.
If you remain silent to me,
I will be like those going down to the Pit.
² Listen to the sound of my pleading
when I cry to you for help,
when I lift up my hands
toward your holy sanctuary.

³ Do not drag me away with the wicked,
with the evildoers,
who speak in friendly ways with their neighbors
while malice is in their hearts.
⁴ Repay them according to what they have done—
according to the evil of their deeds.
Repay them according to the work of their hands;
give them back what they deserve.

It is natural to fixate on your troubles. It is supernatural to look up and seek God amidst those troubles! May your faith-perspective steady you and strengthen others.

⁵ Because they do not consider
what the LORD has done
or the work of his hands,
he will tear them down and not rebuild them.

⁶ Blessed be the LORD,
for he has heard the sound of my pleading.
⁷ The LORD is my strength and my shield;
my heart trusts in him, and I am helped.
Therefore my heart celebrates,
and I give thanks to him with my song.

⁸ The LORD is the strength of his people;
he is a stronghold of salvation for his anointed.
⁹ Save your people, bless your possession,
shepherd them, and carry them forever.

PSALM 29
The Voice of the Lord
A psalm of David.

¹ Ascribe to the LORD, you heavenly beings,
ascribe to the LORD glory and strength.
² Ascribe to the LORD the glory due his name;
worship the LORD
in the splendor of his holiness.

³ The voice of the LORD is above the waters.
The God of glory thunders—
the LORD, above the vast water,
⁴ the voice of the LORD in power,
the voice of the LORD in splendor.
⁵ The voice of the LORD breaks the cedars;
the LORD shatters the cedars of Lebanon.
⁶ He makes Lebanon skip like a calf,
and Sirion, like a young wild ox.
⁷ The voice of the LORD flashes flames of fire.
⁸ The voice of the LORD shakes the wilderness;
the LORD shakes the wilderness of Kadesh.
⁹ The voice of the LORD makes the deer give birth
and strips the woodlands bare.

In his temple all cry, "Glory!"

¹⁰ The LORD sits enthroned over the flood;
the LORD sits enthroned, King forever.
¹¹ The LORD gives his people strength;
the LORD blesses his people with peace.

God is powerful, strong, and true. **And he deeply loves you.** He gives strength. Will you receive it? He gives peace. Will you embrace it?

PSALM 30
Joy in the Morning
A psalm; a dedication song for the house. Of David.

1. I will exalt you, LORD,
because you have lifted me up
and have not allowed my enemies
to triumph over me.
2. LORD my God,
I cried to you for help, and you healed me.
3. LORD, you brought me up from Sheol;
you spared me from among those
going down to the Pit.

4. Sing to the LORD, you his faithful ones,
and praise his holy name.
5. For his anger lasts only a moment,
but his favor, a lifetime.
Weeping may stay overnight,
but there is joy in the morning.

6. When I was secure, I said,
"I will never be shaken."
7. LORD, when you showed your favor,
you made me stand like a strong mountain;
when you hid your face, I was terrified.
8. LORD, I called to you;
I sought favor from my Lord:
9. "What gain is there in my death,
if I go down to the Pit?
Will the dust praise you?
Will it proclaim your truth?
10. LORD, listen and be gracious to me;
LORD, be my helper."

11. You turned my lament into dancing;
you removed my sackcloth
and clothed me with gladness,
12. so that I can sing to you and not be silent.
LORD my God, I will praise you forever.

If you are on the other side of your trial, praise God! And if not, can you thank him by faith? Declare that he has been faithful and will restore you once again.

PSALM 31
A Plea for Protection
For the choir director. A psalm of David.

1 LORD, I seek refuge in you;
let me never be disgraced.
Save me by your righteousness.
2 Listen closely to me; rescue me quickly.
Be a rock of refuge for me,
a mountain fortress to save me.
3 For you are my rock and my fortress;
you lead and guide me
for your name's sake.
4 You will free me from the net
that is secretly set for me,
for you are my refuge.
5 Into your hand I entrust my spirit;
you have redeemed me, LORD, God of truth.
6 I hate those who are devoted to worthless idols,
but I trust in the LORD.
7 I will rejoice and be glad in your faithful love
because you have seen my affliction.
You know the troubles of my soul
8 and have not handed me over to the enemy.
You have set my feet in a spacious place.

9 Be gracious to me, LORD,
because I am in distress;
my eyes are worn out from frustration—
my whole being as well.
10 Indeed, my life is consumed with grief
and my years with groaning;
my strength has failed
because of my iniquity,
and my bones waste away.
11 I am ridiculed by all my adversaries
and even by my neighbors.
I am dreaded by my acquaintances;
those who see me in the street run from me.
12 I am forgotten: gone from memory
like a dead person—like broken pottery.
13 I have heard the gossip of many;
terror is on every side.
When they conspired against me,
they plotted to take my life.

14 But I trust in you, LORD;
I say, "You are my God."
15 The course of my life is in your power;
rescue me from the power of my enemies
and from my persecutors.

God loves it when you look to him for wisdom and direction. In what ways do you need his insight today?

¹⁶ Make your face shine on your servant;
save me by your faithful love.
¹⁷ LORD, do not let me be disgraced when I call on you.
Let the wicked be disgraced;
let them be quiet in Sheol.
¹⁸ Let lying lips
that arrogantly speak against the righteous
in proud contempt be silenced.
¹⁹ How great is your goodness
that you have stored up for those who fear you
and accomplished in the sight of everyone
for those who take refuge in you.
²⁰ You hide them in the protection of your presence;
you conceal them in a shelter
from human schemes,
from quarrelsome tongues.
²¹ Blessed be the LORD,
for he has wondrously shown his faithful love to me
in a city under siege.
²² In my alarm I said,
"I am cut off from your sight."
But you heard the sound of my pleading
when I cried to you for help.

²³ Love the LORD, all his faithful ones.
The LORD protects the loyal,
but fully repays the arrogant.
²⁴ Be strong, and let your heart be courageous,
all you who put your hope in the LORD.

PSALM 32
The Joy of Forgiveness
Of David. A Maskil.

¹ How joyful is the one
whose transgression is forgiven,
whose sin is covered!
² How joyful is a person whom
the LORD does not charge with iniquity
and in whose spirit is no deceit!

³ When I kept silent, my bones became brittle
from my groaning all day long.
⁴ For day and night your hand was heavy on me;
my strength was drained
as in the summer's heat. *Selah*
⁵ Then I acknowledged my sin to you
and did not conceal my iniquity.
I said,
"I will confess my transgressions to the LORD,"
and you forgave the guilt of my sin. *Selah*

Have you condemned yourself for the many ways you fall short? It's time to refuse condemnation. Instead, confess your sins to God. Embrace his grace. And walk free.

⁶ Therefore let everyone who is faithful pray to you immediately.
  When great floodwaters come,
    they will not reach him.
⁷ You are my hiding place;
  you protect me from trouble.
  You surround me with joyful shouts of deliverance.   Selah

⁸ I will instruct you and show you the way to go;
  with my eye on you, I will give counsel.
⁹ Do not be like a horse or mule,
  without understanding,
    that must be controlled with bit and bridle
    or else it will not come near you.

¹⁰ Many pains come to the wicked,
   but the one who trusts in the LORD
     will have faithful love surrounding him.
¹¹ Be glad in the LORD and rejoice,
   you righteous ones;
   shout for joy,
     all you upright in heart.

PSALM 33
Praise to the Creator

¹ Rejoice in the LORD, you righteous ones;
  praise from the upright is beautiful.
² Praise the LORD with the lyre;
  make music to him with a ten-stringed harp.
³ Sing a new song to him;
  play skillfully on the strings, with a joyful shout.

⁴ For the word of the LORD is right,
  and all his work is trustworthy.
⁵ He loves righteousness and justice;
  the earth is full of the LORD's unfailing love.

⁶ The heavens were made by the word of the LORD,
  and all the stars, by the breath of his mouth.
⁷ He gathers the water of the sea into a heap;
  he puts the depths into storehouses.
⁸ Let the whole earth fear the LORD;
  let all the inhabitants of the world stand in awe of him.
⁹ For he spoke, and it came into being;
  he commanded, and it came into existence.

¹⁰ The LORD frustrates the counsel of the nations;
   he thwarts the plans of the peoples.
¹¹ The counsel of the LORD stands forever,
   the plans of his heart from generation to generation.
¹² Happy is the nation whose God is the LORD—
   the people he has chosen to be his own possession!

God's Word is an anchor. His heart is good. Tether your problems to his promises today. It is impossible for him to fail you.

¹³ The LORD looks down from heaven;
he observes everyone.
¹⁴ He gazes on all the inhabitants of the earth
from his dwelling place.
¹⁵ He forms the hearts of them all;
he considers all their works.
¹⁶ A king is not saved by a large army;
a warrior will not be rescued by great strength.
¹⁷ The horse is a false hope for safety;
it provides no escape by its great power.

¹⁸ But look, the LORD keeps his eye on those who fear him—
those who depend on his faithful love
¹⁹ to rescue them from death
and to keep them alive in famine.

²⁰ We wait for the LORD;
he is our help and shield.
²¹ For our hearts rejoice in him
because we trust in his holy name.
²² May your faithful love rest on us, LORD,
for we put our hope in you.

PSALM 34
The Lord Delivers the Righteous

Concerning David, when he pretended to be insane in the presence of Abimelech, who drove him out, and he departed.

¹ I will bless the LORD at all times;
his praise will always be on my lips.
² I will boast in the LORD;
the humble will hear and be glad.
³ Proclaim the LORD's greatness with me;
let us exalt his name together.

⁴ I sought the LORD, and he answered me
and rescued me from all my fears.
⁵ Those who look to him are radiant with joy;
their faces will never be ashamed.
⁶ This poor man cried, and the LORD heard him
and saved him from all his troubles.
⁷ The angel of the LORD encamps
around those who fear him, and rescues them.

⁸ Taste and see that the LORD is good.
How happy is the person who takes refuge in him!
⁹ You who are his holy ones, fear the LORD,
for those who fear him lack nothing.
¹⁰ Young lions lack food and go hungry,
but those who seek the LORD
will not lack any good thing.

There is no fear, shame, or worry in Jesus' heart. When you look *to* him, you begin to look *like* him. How has he changed your life thus far?

¹¹ Come, children, listen to me;
I will teach you the fear of the LORD.
¹² Who is someone who desires life,
loving a long life to enjoy what is good?
¹³ Keep your tongue from evil
and your lips from deceitful speech.
¹⁴ Turn away from evil and do what is good;
seek peace and pursue it.

¹⁵ The eyes of the LORD are on the righteous,
and his ears are open to their cry for help.
¹⁶ The face of the LORD is set
against those who do what is evil,
to remove all memory of them from the earth.
¹⁷ The righteous cry out, and the LORD hears,
and rescues them from all their troubles.
¹⁸ The LORD is near the brokenhearted;
he saves those crushed in spirit.

¹⁹ One who is righteous has many adversities,
but the LORD rescues him from them all.
²⁰ He protects all his bones;
not one of them is broken.
²¹ Evil brings death to the wicked,
and those who hate the righteous will be punished.
²² The LORD redeems the life of his servants,
and all who take refuge in him will not be punished.

PSALM 35
Prayer for Victory
Of David.

¹ Oppose my opponents, LORD;
fight those who fight me.
² Take your shields—large and small—
and come to my aid.
³ Draw the spear and javelin against my pursuers,
and assure me: "I am your deliverance."

⁴ Let those who intend to take my life
be disgraced and humiliated;
let those who plan to harm me
be turned back and ashamed.
⁵ Let them be like chaff in the wind,
with the angel of the LORD driving them away.
⁶ Let their way be dark and slippery,
with the angel of the LORD pursuing them.
⁷ They hid their net for me without cause;
they dug a pit for me without cause.
⁸ Let ruin come on him unexpectedly,
and let the net that he hid ensnare him;
let him fall into it—to his ruin.

The wicked prosper when the godly do nothing. Stand in the gap and pray that the schemes of the wicked will come to nothing.

⁹ Then I will rejoice in the LORD;
I will delight in his deliverance.
¹⁰ All my bones will say,
"LORD, who is like you,
rescuing the poor from one too strong for him,
the poor or the needy from one who robs him?"

¹¹ Malicious witnesses come forward;
they question me about things I do not know.
¹² They repay me evil for good,
making me desolate.
¹³ Yet when they were sick,
my clothing was sackcloth;
I humbled myself with fasting,
and my prayer was genuine.
¹⁴ I went about mourning as if for my friend or brother;
I was bowed down with grief,
like one mourning for a mother.
¹⁵ But when I stumbled, they gathered in glee;
they gathered against me.
Assailants I did not know
tore at me and did not stop.
¹⁶ With godless mockery
they gnashed their teeth at me.

¹⁷ Lord, how long will you look on?
Rescue me from their ravages;
rescue my precious life from the young lions.
¹⁸ I will praise you in the great assembly;
I will exalt you among many people.
¹⁹ Do not let my deceitful enemies rejoice over me;
do not let those who hate me without cause
wink at me maliciously.
²⁰ For they do not speak in friendly ways,
but contrive fraudulent schemes
against those who live peacefully in the land.
²¹ They open their mouths wide against me and say,
"Aha, aha! We saw it!"

²² You saw it, LORD; do not be silent.
Lord, do not be far from me.
²³ Wake up and rise to my defense,
to my cause, my God and my Lord!
²⁴ Vindicate me, LORD my God,
in keeping with your righteousness,
and do not let them rejoice over me.
²⁵ Do not let them say in their hearts,
"Aha! Just what we wanted."
Do not let them say,
"We have swallowed him up!"

26 Let those who rejoice at my misfortune
be disgraced and humiliated;
let those who exalt themselves over me
be clothed with shame and reproach.

27 Let those who want my vindication
shout for joy and be glad;
let them continually say,
"The LORD be exalted.
He takes pleasure in his servant's well-being."
28 And my tongue will proclaim your righteousness,
your praise all day long.

PSALM 36
Human Wickedness and God's Love
For the choir director. Of David, the Lord's servant.

1 An oracle within my heart
concerning the transgression of the wicked person:
Dread of God has no effect on him.
2 For with his flattering opinion of himself,
he does not discover and hate his iniquity.
3 The words from his mouth are malicious and deceptive;
he has stopped acting wisely and doing good.
4 Even on his bed he makes malicious plans.
He sets himself on a path that is not good,
and he does not reject evil.

5 LORD, your faithful love reaches to heaven,
your faithfulness to the clouds.
6 Your righteousness is like the highest mountains,
your judgments like the deepest sea.
LORD, you preserve people and animals.
7 How priceless your faithful love is, God!
People take refuge in the shadow of your wings.
8 They are filled from the abundance of your house.
You let them drink from your refreshing stream.
9 For the wellspring of life is with you.
By means of your light we see light.

10 Spread your faithful love over those who know you,
and your righteousness over the upright in heart.
11 Do not let the foot of the arrogant come near me
or the hand of the wicked drive me away.
12 There! The evildoers have fallen.
They have been thrown down and cannot rise.

Whenever the enemy makes a move, stand in faith, because God already has a plan. Declare God's greatness over your battle today!

PSALM 37
Instruction in Wisdom
Of David.

1. Do not be agitated by evildoers;
   do not envy those who do wrong.
2. For they wither quickly like grass
   and wilt like tender green plants.
3. Trust in the LORD and do what is good;
   dwell in the land and live securely.
4. Take delight in the LORD,
   and he will give you your heart's desires.
5. Commit your way to the LORD;
   trust in him, and he will act,
6. making your righteousness shine like the dawn,
   your justice like the noonday.
7. Be silent before the LORD and wait expectantly for him;
   do not be agitated by one who prospers in his way,
   by the person who carries out evil plans.
8. Refrain from anger and give up your rage;
   do not be agitated—it can only bring harm.
9. For evildoers will be destroyed,
   but those who put their hope in the LORD
   will inherit the land.
10. A little while, and the wicked person will be no more;
    though you look for him, he will not be there.
11. But the humble will inherit the land
    and will enjoy abundant prosperity.
12. The wicked person schemes against the righteous
    and gnashes his teeth at him.
13. The Lord laughs at him
    because he sees that his day is coming.
14. The wicked have drawn the sword and strung the bow
    to bring down the poor and needy
    and to slaughter those whose way is upright.
15. Their swords will enter their own hearts,
    and their bows will be broken.
16. The little that the righteous person has is better
    than the abundance of many wicked people.
17. For the arms of the wicked will be broken,
    but the LORD supports the righteous.
18. The LORD watches over the blameless all their days,
    and their inheritance will last forever.
19. They will not be disgraced in times of adversity;
    they will be satisfied in days of hunger.

Those who delight in the Lord are firmly established in him. What will you entrust to him?

²⁰ But the wicked will perish;
the LORD's enemies, like the glory of the pastures,
will fade away—
they will fade away like smoke.

²¹ The wicked person borrows and does not repay,
but the righteous one is gracious and giving.
²² Those who are blessed by the LORD will inherit the land,
but those cursed by him will be destroyed.

²³ A person's steps are established by the LORD,
and he takes pleasure in his way.
²⁴ Though he falls, he will not be overwhelmed,
because the LORD supports him with his hand.

²⁵ I have been young and now I am old,
yet I have not seen the righteous abandoned
or his children begging for bread.
²⁶ He is always generous, always lending,
and his children are a blessing.

²⁷ Turn away from evil, do what is good,
and settle permanently.
²⁸ For the LORD loves justice
and will not abandon his faithful ones.
They are kept safe forever,
but the children of the wicked will be destroyed.
²⁹ The righteous will inherit the land
and dwell in it permanently.

³⁰ The mouth of the righteous utters wisdom;
his tongue speaks what is just.
³¹ The instruction of his God is in his heart;
his steps do not falter.

³² The wicked one lies in wait for the righteous
and intends to kill him;
³³ the LORD will not leave him
in the power of the wicked one
or allow him to be condemned when he is judged.

³⁴ Wait for the LORD and keep his way,
and he will exalt you to inherit the land.
You will watch when the wicked are destroyed.

³⁵ I have seen a wicked, violent person
well-rooted, like a flourishing native tree.
³⁶ Then I passed by and noticed he was gone;
I searched for him, but he could not be found.

³⁷ Watch the blameless and observe the upright,
for the person of peace will have a future.
³⁸ But transgressors will all be eliminated;
the future of the wicked will be destroyed.

³⁹ The salvation of the righteous is from the LORD,
their refuge in a time of distress.
⁴⁰ The LORD helps and delivers them;
he will deliver them from the wicked and will save them
because they take refuge in him.

PSALM 38
Prayer of a Suffering Sinner
A psalm of David for remembrance.

¹ LORD, do not punish me in your anger
or discipline me in your wrath.
² For your arrows have sunk into me,
and your hand has pressed down on me.

³ There is no soundness in my body
because of your indignation;
there is no health in my bones
because of my sin.
⁴ For my iniquities have flooded over my head;
they are a burden too heavy for me to bear.
⁵ My wounds are foul and festering
because of my foolishness.
⁶ I am bent over and brought very low;
all day long I go around in mourning.
⁷ For my insides are full of burning pain,
and there is no soundness in my body.
⁸ I am faint and severely crushed;
I groan because of the anguish of my heart.

⁹ Lord, my every desire is in front of you;
my sighing is not hidden from you.
¹⁰ My heart races, my strength leaves me,
and even the light of my eyes has faded.
¹¹ My loved ones and friends stand back from my affliction,
and my relatives stand at a distance.
¹² Those who intend to kill me set traps,
and those who want to harm me threaten to destroy me;
they plot treachery all day long.

¹³ I am like a deaf person; I do not hear.
I am like a speechless person
who does not open his mouth.
¹⁴ I am like a man who does not hear
and has no arguments in his mouth.
¹⁵ For I put my hope in you, LORD;
you will answer me, my Lord, my God.
¹⁶ For I said, "Don't let them rejoice over me—
those who are arrogant toward me when I stumble."
¹⁷ For I am about to fall,
and my pain is constantly with me.

We are desperate for God whether we know it or not. Confess your need for him today. And the good news? He is right here.

¹⁸ So I confess my iniquity;
   I am anxious because of my sin.
¹⁹ But my enemies are vigorous and powerful;
   many hate me for no reason.
²⁰ Those who repay evil for good
   attack me for pursuing good.

²¹ LORD, do not abandon me;
   my God, do not be far from me.
²² Hurry to help me,
   my Lord, my salvation.

PSALM 39
The Fleeting Nature of Life
For the choir director, for Jeduthun. A psalm of David.

¹ I said, "I will guard my ways
   so that I may not sin with my tongue;
   I will guard my mouth with a muzzle
   as long as the wicked are in my presence."
² I was speechless and quiet;
   I kept silent, even from speaking good,
   and my pain intensified.
³ My heart grew hot within me;
   as I mused, a fire burned.
   I spoke with my tongue:
⁴ "LORD, make me aware of my end
   and the number of my days
   so that I will know how short-lived I am.
⁵ In fact, you have made my days just inches long,
   and my life span is as nothing to you.
   Yes, every human being stands as only a vapor.   *Selah*
⁶ Yes, a person goes about like a mere shadow.
   Indeed, they rush around in vain,
   gathering possessions
   without knowing who will get them.

⁷ "Now, Lord, what do I wait for?
   My hope is in you.
⁸ Rescue me from all my transgressions;
   do not make me the taunt of fools.
⁹ I am speechless; I do not open my mouth
   because of what you have done.
¹⁰ Remove your torment from me.
   Because of the force of your hand I am finished.
¹¹ You discipline a person with punishment for iniquity,
   consuming like a moth what is precious to him;
   yes, every human being is only a vapor.   *Selah*

We so quickly shift our trust from God to earthly things. Is it your efforts? Your finances? Your appearance? Your relationships? Reset your course today.

¹² "Hear my prayer, LORD,
and listen to my cry for help;
do not be silent at my tears.
For I am here with you as an alien,
a temporary resident like all my ancestors.
¹³ Turn your angry gaze from me
so that I may be cheered up
before I die and am gone."

PSALM 40
Thanksgiving and a Cry for Help
For the choir director. A psalm of David.

¹ I waited patiently for the LORD,
and he turned to me and heard my cry for help.
² He brought me up from a desolate pit,
out of the muddy clay,
and set my feet on a rock,
making my steps secure.
³ He put a new song in my mouth,
a hymn of praise to our God.
Many will see and fear,
and they will trust in the LORD.

⁴ How happy is anyone
who has put his trust in the LORD
and has not turned to the proud
or to those who run after lies!
⁵ LORD my God, you have done many things—
your wondrous works and your plans for us;
none can compare with you.
If I were to report and speak of them,
they are more than can be told.

⁶ You do not delight in sacrifice and offering;
you open my ears to listen.
You do not ask for a whole burnt offering or a sin offering.
⁷ Then I said, "See, I have come;
in the scroll it is written about me.
⁸ I delight to do your will, my God,
and your instruction is deep within me."

⁹ I proclaim righteousness in the great assembly;
see, I do not keep my mouth closed—
as you know, LORD.
¹⁰ I did not hide your righteousness in my heart;
I spoke about your faithfulness and salvation;
I did not conceal your constant love and truth
from the great assembly.

¹¹ LORD, you do not withhold your compassion from me.
Your constant love and truth will always guard me.

You waited on God. He answered. What has God accomplished in your life? How have you seen him break through?

¹² For troubles without number have surrounded me;
   my iniquities have overtaken me; I am unable to see.
   They are more than the hairs of my head,
   and my courage leaves me.
¹³ LORD, be pleased to rescue me;
   hurry to help me, LORD.

¹⁴ Let those who intend to take my life
   be disgraced and confounded.
   Let those who wish me harm
   be turned back and humiliated.
¹⁵ Let those who say to me, "Aha, aha!"
   be appalled because of their shame.

¹⁶ Let all who seek you rejoice and be glad in you;
   let those who love your salvation continually say,
   "The LORD is great!"
¹⁷ I am oppressed and needy;
   may the Lord think of me.
   You are my helper and my deliverer;
   my God, do not delay.

PSALM 41
Victory in Spite of Betrayal
For the choir director. A psalm of David.

¹ Happy is one who is considerate of the poor;
  the LORD will save him in a day of adversity.
² The LORD will keep him and preserve him;
  he will be blessed in the land.
  You will not give him over to the desire of his enemies.
³ The LORD will sustain him on his sickbed;
  you will heal him on the bed where he lies.

⁴ I said, "LORD, be gracious to me;
  heal me, for I have sinned against you."
⁵ My enemies speak maliciously about me:
  "When will he die and be forgotten?"
⁶ When one of them comes to visit, he speaks deceitfully;
  he stores up evil in his heart;
  he goes out and talks.
⁷ All who hate me whisper together about me;
  they plan to harm me.
⁸ "Something awful has overwhelmed him,
  and he won't rise again from where he lies!"
⁹ Even my friend in whom I trusted,
  one who ate my bread,
  has raised his heel against me.

¹⁰ But you, LORD, be gracious to me and raise me up;
   then I will repay them.

We sometimes fail others. They fail us. We need God's grace and mercy. Entrust your relationships and your identity to him.

11 By this I know that you delight in me:
my enemy does not shout in triumph over me.
12 You supported me because of my integrity
and set me in your presence forever.

13 Blessed be the LORD God of Israel,
from everlasting to everlasting.
Amen and amen.

PSALM 42
Longing for God
For the choir director. A Maskil of the sons of Korah.

1 As a deer longs for flowing streams,
so I long for you, God.
2 I thirst for God, the living God.
When can I come and appear before God?
3 My tears have been my food day and night,
while all day long people say to me,
"Where is your God?"
4 I remember this as I pour out my heart:
how I walked with many,
leading the festive procession to the house of God,
with joyful and thankful shouts.

5 Why, my soul, are you so dejected?
Why are you in such turmoil?
Put your hope in God, for I will still praise him,
my Savior and my God.
6 I am deeply depressed;
therefore I remember you from the land of Jordan
and the peaks of Hermon, from Mount Mizar.
7 Deep calls to deep in the roar of your waterfalls;
all your breakers and your billows have swept over me.
8 The LORD will send his faithful love by day;
his song will be with me in the night—
a prayer to the God of my life.

9 I will say to God, my rock,
"Why have you forgotten me?
Why must I go about in sorrow
because of the enemy's oppression?"
10 My adversaries taunt me,
as if crushing my bones,
while all day long they say to me,
"Where is your God?"
11 Why, my soul, are you so dejected?
Why are you in such turmoil?
Put your hope in God, for I will still praise him,
my Savior and my God.

Sometimes we need to speak life and strength to our souls. What does your soul need to hear today?

PSALM 43

1 Vindicate me, God, and champion my cause
against an unfaithful nation;
rescue me from the deceitful and unjust person.
2 For you are the God of my refuge.
Why have you rejected me?
Why must I go about in sorrow
because of the enemy's oppression?

3 Send your light and your truth; let them lead me.
Let them bring me to your holy mountain,
to your dwelling place.
4 Then I will come to the altar of God,
to God, my greatest joy.
I will praise you with the lyre,
God, my God.

5 Why, my soul, are you so dejected?
Why are you in such turmoil?
Put your hope in God, for I will still praise him,
my Savior and my God.

PSALM 44
Israel's Complaint
For the choir director. A Maskil of the sons of Korah.

1 God, we have heard with our ears—
our ancestors have told us—
the work you accomplished in their days,
in days long ago:
2 In order to plant them,
you displaced the nations by your hand;
in order to settle them,
you brought disaster on the peoples.
3 For they did not take the land by their sword—
their arm did not bring them victory—
but by your right hand, your arm,
and the light of your face,
because you were favorable toward them.

4 You are my King, my God,
who ordains victories for Jacob.
5 Through you we drive back our foes;
through your name we trample our enemies.
6 For I do not trust in my bow,
and my sword does not bring me victory.
7 But you give us victory over our foes
and let those who hate us be disgraced.
8 We boast in God all day long;
we will praise your name forever.   *Selah*

God defends and delivers. He rescues and redeems. What do you need to remember about God? _____

_____
_____
_____
_____
_____
_____

We cannot win battles in our own strength. We need God's favor, his power, and his smile over our lives if we hope to stand in victory. Seek his favor afresh today. _____

_____
_____
_____
_____
_____
_____
_____

9 But you have rejected and humiliated us;
   you do not march out with our armies.
10 You make us retreat from the foe,
   and those who hate us
   have taken plunder for themselves.
11 You hand us over to be eaten like sheep
   and scatter us among the nations.
12 You sell your people for nothing;
   you make no profit from selling them.
13 You make us an object of reproach to our neighbors,
   a source of mockery and ridicule to those around us.
14 You make us a joke among the nations,
   a laughingstock among the peoples.
15 My disgrace is before me all day long,
   and shame has covered my face,
16 because of the taunts of the scorner and reviler,
   because of the enemy and avenger.

17 All this has happened to us,
   but we have not forgotten you
   or betrayed your covenant.
18 Our hearts have not turned back;
   our steps have not strayed from your path.
19 But you have crushed us in a haunt of jackals
   and have covered us with deepest darkness.
20 If we had forgotten the name of our God
   and spread out our hands to a foreign god,
21 wouldn't God have found this out,
   since he knows the secrets of the heart?
22 Because of you we are being put to death all day long;
   we are counted as sheep to be slaughtered.

23 Wake up, LORD! Why are you sleeping?
   Get up! Don't reject us forever!
24 Why do you hide
   and forget our affliction and oppression?
25 For we have sunk down to the dust;
   our bodies cling to the ground.
26 Rise up! Help us!
   Redeem us because of your faithful love.

PSALM 45
A Royal Wedding Song
For the choir director: according to "The Lilies." A Maskil of the sons of Korah. A love song.

1 My heart is moved by a noble theme
  as I recite my verses to the king;
  my tongue is the pen of a skillful writer.
2 You are the most handsome of men;
  grace flows from your lips.
  Therefore God has blessed you forever.

God is truth, humility, and justice. **And he greatly uses** those who share his passion. How is he calling you upward in truth, humility, and justice?

³ Mighty warrior, strap your sword at your side.
In your majesty and splendor—
⁴ in your splendor ride triumphantly
in the cause of truth, humility, and justice.
May your right hand show your awe-inspiring acts.
⁵ Your sharpened arrows pierce the hearts of the king's enemies;
the peoples fall under you.

⁶ Your throne, God, is forever and ever;
the scepter of your kingdom is a scepter of justice.
⁷ You love righteousness and hate wickedness;
therefore God, your God, has anointed you with the oil of joy
more than your companions.
⁸ Myrrh, aloes, and cassia perfume all your garments;
from ivory palaces harps bring you joy.
⁹ Kings' daughters are among your honored women;
the queen, adorned with gold from Ophir,
stands at your right hand.

¹⁰ Listen, daughter, pay attention and consider:
forget your people and your father's house,
¹¹ and the king will desire your beauty.
Bow down to him, for he is your lord.
¹² The daughter of Tyre, the wealthy people,
will seek your favor with gifts.

¹³ In her chamber, the royal daughter is all glorious,
her clothing embroidered with gold.
¹⁴ In colorful garments she is led to the king;
after her, the virgins, her companions, are brought to you.
¹⁵ They are led in with gladness and rejoicing;
they enter the king's palace.
¹⁶ Your sons will succeed your ancestors;
you will make them princes throughout the land.
¹⁷ I will cause your name to be remembered for all generations;
therefore the peoples will praise you forever and ever.

PSALM 46
God Our Refuge

For the choir director. A song of the sons of Korah. According to Alamoth.

¹ God is our refuge and strength,
a helper who is always found
in times of trouble.
² Therefore we will not be afraid,
though the earth trembles
and the mountains topple
into the depths of the seas,
³ though its water roars and foams
and the mountains quake with its turmoil.   *Selah*

We forget about God's power when we strive and strain through life. Those areas of soul-unrest? Ask for a fresh sense of his power and strength, and then watch him work.

4 There is a river—
its streams delight the city of God,
the holy dwelling place of the Most High.
5 God is within her; she will not be toppled.
God will help her when the morning dawns.
6 Nations rage, kingdoms topple;
the earth melts when he lifts his voice.
7 The LORD of Armies is with us;
the God of Jacob is our stronghold. Selah

8 Come, see the works of the LORD,
who brings devastation on the earth.
9 He makes wars cease throughout the earth.
He shatters bows and cuts spears to pieces;
he sets wagons ablaze.
10 "Stop your fighting, and know that I am God,
exalted among the nations, exalted on the earth."
11 The LORD of Armies is with us;
the God of Jacob is our stronghold. Selah

PSALM 47
God Our King
For the choir director. A psalm of the sons of Korah.

1 Clap your hands, all you peoples;
shout to God with a jubilant cry.
2 For the LORD, the Most High, is awe-inspiring,
a great King over the whole earth.
3 He subdues peoples under us
and nations under our feet.
4 He chooses for us our inheritance—
the pride of Jacob, whom he loves. Selah

5 God ascends among shouts of joy,
the LORD, with the sound of trumpets.
6 Sing praise to God, sing praise;
sing praise to our King, sing praise!
7 Sing a song of wisdom,
for God is King of the whole earth.

8 God reigns over the nations;
God is seated on his holy throne.
9 The nobles of the peoples have assembled
with the people of the God of Abraham.
For the leaders of the earth belong to God;
he is greatly exalted.

Praise God with a song today. **Write out your own** declaration of his greatness and power.

PSALM 48
Zion Exalted
A song. A psalm of the sons of Korah.

1 The Lord is great and highly praised
in the city of our God.
His holy mountain, 2 rising splendidly,
is the joy of the whole earth.
Mount Zion—the summit of Zaphon—
is the city of the great King.
3 God is known as a stronghold
in its citadels.

4 Look! The kings assembled;
they advanced together.
5 They looked and froze with fear;
they fled in terror.
6 Trembling seized them there,
agony like that of a woman in labor,
7 as you wrecked the ships of Tarshish
with the east wind.
8 Just as we heard, so we have seen
in the city of the LORD of Armies,
in the city of our God;
God will establish it forever.   *Selah*

9 God, within your temple,
we contemplate your faithful love.
10 Like your name, God, so your praise
reaches to the ends of the earth;
your right hand is filled with justice.
11 Mount Zion is glad.
Judah's villages rejoice
because of your judgments.

12 Go around Zion, encircle it;
count its towers,
13 note its ramparts; tour its citadels
so that you can tell a future generation:
14 "This God, our God forever and ever—
he will always lead us."

PSALM 49
Misplaced Trust in Wealth
For the choir director. A psalm of the sons of Korah.

1 Hear this, all you peoples;
listen, all who inhabit the world,
2 both low and high,
rich and poor together.
3 My mouth speaks wisdom;
my heart's meditation brings understanding.

There is no one like our God. What he builds cannot be destroyed. He guards, he guides, he purposes, and he provides. Seek his wisdom in your endeavors.

⁴ I turn my ear to a proverb;
   I explain my riddle with a lyre.

⁵ Why should I fear in times of trouble?
   The iniquity of my foes surrounds me.
⁶ They trust in their wealth
   and boast of their abundant riches.
⁷ Yet these cannot redeem a person
   or pay his ransom to God—
⁸ since the price of redeeming him is too costly,
   one should forever stop trying—
⁹ so that he may live forever
   and not see the Pit.

¹⁰ For one can see that the wise die;
   the foolish and stupid also pass away.
   Then they leave their wealth to others.
¹¹ Their graves are their permanent homes,
   their dwellings from generation to generation,
   though they have named estates after themselves.
¹² But despite his assets, mankind will not last;
   he is like the animals that perish.

¹³ This is the way of those who are arrogant,
   and of their followers,
   who approve of their words.   *Selah*
¹⁴ Like sheep they are headed for Sheol;
   Death will shepherd them.
   The upright will rule over them in the morning,
   and their form will waste away in Sheol,
   far from their lofty abode.
¹⁵ But God will redeem me
   from the power of Sheol,
   for he will take me.   *Selah*

¹⁶ Do not be afraid when a person gets rich,
   when the wealth of his house increases.
¹⁷ For when he dies, he will take nothing at all;
   his wealth will not follow him down.
¹⁸ Though he blesses himself during his lifetime—
   and you are acclaimed when you do well for yourself—
¹⁹ he will go to the generation of his fathers;
   they will never see the light.
²⁰ Mankind, with his assets
   but without understanding,
   is like the animals that perish.

Life on earth is short. Eternity is long. Look to the One who holds your inheritance. What is he saying to you today?

PSALM 50
God as Judge
A psalm of Asaph.

1. The Mighty One, God, the LORD, speaks;
   he summons the earth
   from the rising of the sun to its setting.
2. From Zion, the perfection of beauty,
   God appears in radiance.
3. Our God is coming; he will not be silent!
   Devouring fire precedes him,
   and a storm rages around him.
4. On high, he summons heaven and earth
   in order to judge his people:
5. "Gather my faithful ones to me,
   those who made a covenant with me by sacrifice."
6. The heavens proclaim his righteousness,
   for God is the Judge.   *Selah*

7. "Listen, my people, and I will speak;
   I will testify against you, Israel.
   I am God, your God.
8. I do not rebuke you for your sacrifices
   or for your burnt offerings,
   which are continually before me.
9. I will not take a bull from your household
   or male goats from your pens,
10. for every animal of the forest is mine,
    the cattle on a thousand hills.
11. I know every bird of the mountains,
    and the creatures of the field are mine.
12. If I were hungry, I would not tell you,
    for the world and everything in it is mine.
13. Do I eat the flesh of bulls
    or drink the blood of goats?
14. Sacrifice a thank offering to God,
    and pay your vows to the Most High.
15. Call on me in a day of trouble;
    I will rescue you, and you will honor me."

16. But God says to the wicked:
    "What right do you have to recite my statutes
    and to take my covenant on your lips?
17. You hate instruction
    and fling my words behind you.
18. When you see a thief,
    you make friends with him,
    and you associate with adulterers.
19. You unleash your mouth for evil
    and harness your tongue for deceit.

God is not impressed or blessed by our striving and straining. What he loves is a grateful, obedient heart. Give him thanks today. And determine to obey him, even when it doesn't suit you.

²⁰ You sit, maligning your brother,
slandering your mother's son.
²¹ You have done these things, and I kept silent;
you thought I was just like you.
But I will rebuke you
and lay out the case before you.

²² "Understand this, you who forget God,
or I will tear you apart,
and there will be no one to rescue you.
²³ Whoever sacrifices a thank offering honors me,
and whoever orders his conduct,
I will show him the salvation of God."

PSALM 51
A Prayer for Restoration

For the choir director. A psalm of David, when the prophet Nathan came to him after he had gone to Bathsheba.

¹ Be gracious to me, God,
according to your faithful love;
according to your abundant compassion,
blot out my rebellion.
² Completely wash away my guilt
and cleanse me from my sin.
³ For I am conscious of my rebellion,
and my sin is always before me.
⁴ Against you—you alone—I have sinned
and done this evil in your sight.
So you are right when you pass sentence;
you are blameless when you judge.
⁵ Indeed, I was guilty when I was born;
I was sinful when my mother conceived me.

⁶ Surely you desire integrity in the inner self,
and you teach me wisdom deep within.
⁷ Purify me with hyssop, and I will be clean;
wash me, and I will be whiter than snow.
⁸ Let me hear joy and gladness;
let the bones you have crushed rejoice.
⁹ Turn your face away from my sins
and blot out all my guilt.
¹⁰ God, create a clean heart for me
and renew a steadfast spirit within me.
¹¹ Do not banish me from your presence
or take your Holy Spirit from me.
¹² Restore the joy of your salvation to me,
and sustain me by giving me a willing spirit.
¹³ Then I will teach the rebellious your ways,
and sinners will return to you.

God wants truth in our inmost being because that is where most lies go to hide. Wait on the Lord. Ask him to uproot the lies and to deeply sow seeds of truth.

14 Save me from the guilt of bloodshed, God—
   God of my salvation—
   and my tongue will sing of your righteousness.
15 Lord, open my lips,
   and my mouth will declare your praise.
16 You do not want a sacrifice, or I would give it;
   you are not pleased with a burnt offering.
17 The sacrifice pleasing to God is a broken spirit.
   You will not despise a broken and humbled heart, God.

18 In your good pleasure, cause Zion to prosper;
   build the walls of Jerusalem.
19 Then you will delight in righteous sacrifices,
   whole burnt offerings;
   then bulls will be offered on your altar.

PSALM 52
God Judges the Proud

For the choir director. A Maskil of David. When Doeg the Edomite went and reported to Saul, telling him, "David went to Ahimelech's house."

1 Why boast about evil, you hero!
   God's faithful love is constant.
2 Like a sharpened razor,
   your tongue devises destruction,
   working treachery.
3 You love evil instead of good,
   lying instead of speaking truthfully.   *Selah*
4 You love any words that destroy,
   you treacherous tongue!
5 This is why God will bring you down forever.
   He will take you, ripping you out of your tent;
   he will uproot you from the land of the living.   *Selah*
6 The righteous will see and fear,
   and they will derisively say about that hero,
7 "Here is the man
   who would not make God his refuge,
   but trusted in the abundance of his riches,
   taking refuge in his destructive behavior."

8 But I am like a flourishing olive tree
   in the house of God;
   I trust in God's faithful love forever and ever.
9 I will praise you forever for what you have done.
   In the presence of your faithful people,
   I will put my hope in your name, for it is good.

From all appearances, the wicked seem to thrive. But the truth is, God's people have his promises and his presence. Ask him to renew your perspective today.

PSALM 53
A Portrait of Sinners
For the choir director: on Mahalath. A Maskil of David.

1. The fool says in his heart, "There's no God."
   They are corrupt, and they do vile deeds.
   There is no one who does good.
2. God looks down from heaven on the human race
   to see if there is one who is wise,
   one who seeks God.
3. All have turned away;
   all alike have become corrupt.
   There is no one who does good,
   not even one.

4. Will evildoers never understand?
   They consume my people as they consume bread;
   they do not call on God.
5. Then they will be filled with dread—
   dread like no other—
   because God will scatter
   the bones of those who besiege you.
   You will put them to shame,
   for God has rejected them.

6. Oh, that Israel's deliverance would come from Zion!
   When God restores the fortunes of his people,
   let Jacob rejoice, let Israel be glad.

PSALM 54
Prayer for Deliverance
For the choir director: with stringed instruments. A Maskil of David. When the Ziphites went and said to Saul, "Is David not hiding among us?"

1. God, save me by your name,
   and vindicate me by your might!
2. God, hear my prayer;
   listen to the words from my mouth.
3. For strangers rise up against me,
   and violent men intend to kill me.
   They do not let God guide them.   *Selah*

4. God is my helper;
   the Lord is the sustainer of my life.
5. He will repay my adversaries for their evil.
   Because of your faithfulness, annihilate them.

6. I will sacrifice a freewill offering to you.
   I will praise your name, LORD,
   because it is good.
7. For he has rescued me from every trouble,
   and my eye has looked down on my enemies.

The fool says in his heart that there is no God. But there is! And he lives! What are you believing God for today? _____

_____

_____

_____

_____

_____

_____

God is your helper, and he will come through for you! Write a declaration of victory today. Write it before the breakthrough comes. It will strengthen your faith. _____

_____

_____

_____

_____

_____

_____

PSALM 55
Betrayal by a Friend
For the choir director: with stringed instruments. A Maskil of David.

1 God, listen to my prayer
and do not hide from my plea for help.
2 Pay attention to me and answer me.
I am restless and in turmoil with my complaint,
3 because of the enemy's words,
because of the pressure of the wicked.
For they bring down disaster on me
and harass me in anger.

4 My heart shudders within me;
terrors of death sweep over me.
5 Fear and trembling grip me;
horror has overwhelmed me.
6 I said, "If only I had wings like a dove!
I would fly away and find rest.
7 How far away I would flee;
I would stay in the wilderness.   *Selah*
8 I would hurry to my shelter
from the raging wind and the storm."

9 Lord, confuse and confound their speech,
for I see violence and strife in the city;
10 day and night they make the rounds on its walls.
Crime and trouble are within it;
11 destruction is inside it;
oppression and deceit never leave its marketplace.

12 Now it is not an enemy who insults me—
otherwise I could bear it;
it is not a foe who rises up against me—
otherwise I could hide from him.
13 But it is you, a man who is my peer,
my companion and good friend!
14 We used to have close fellowship;
we walked with the crowd into the house of God.

15 Let death take them by surprise;
let them go down to Sheol alive,
because evil is in their homes and within them.
16 But I call to God,
and the LORD will save me.
17 I complain and groan morning, noon, and night,
and he hears my voice.
18 Though many are against me,
he will redeem me from my battle unharmed.
19 God, the one enthroned from long ago,
will hear and will humiliate them   *Selah*
because they do not change
and do not fear God.

Give your burdens to the Lord today. He will take care of you.

²⁰ My friend acts violently
against those at peace with him;
he violates his covenant.
²¹ His buttery words are smooth,
but war is in his heart.
His words are softer than oil,
but they are drawn swords.

²² Cast your burden on the LORD,
and he will sustain you;
he will never allow the righteous to be shaken.

²³ God, you will bring them down
to the Pit of destruction;
men of bloodshed and treachery
will not live out half their days.
But I will trust in you.

PSALM 56
A Call for God's Protection

For the choir director: according to "A Silent Dove Far Away." A Miktam of David. When the Philistines seized him in Gath.

¹ Be gracious to me, God, for a man is trampling me;
he fights and oppresses me all day long.
² My adversaries trample me all day,
for many arrogantly fight against me.
³ When I am afraid,
I will trust in you.
⁴ In God, whose word I praise,
in God I trust; I will not be afraid.
What can mere mortals do to me?

⁵ They twist my words all day long;
all their thoughts against me are evil.
⁶ They stir up strife, they lurk;
they watch my steps
while they wait to take my life.
⁷ Will they escape in spite of such sin?
God, bring down the nations in wrath.

⁸ You yourself have recorded my wanderings.
Put my tears in your bottle.
Are they not in your book?
⁹ Then my enemies will retreat on the day when I call.
This I know: God is for me.

¹⁰ In God, whose word I praise,
in the LORD, whose word I praise,
¹¹ in God I trust; I will not be afraid.
What can mere humans do to me?

Which of God's promises mean the most to you right now?

¹² I am obligated by vows to you, God;
   I will make my thank offerings to you.
¹³ For you rescued me from death,
   even my feet from stumbling,
   to walk before God in the light of life.

PSALM 57
Praise for God's Protection
For the choir director: "Do Not Destroy." A Miktam of David. When he fled before Saul into the cave.

¹ Be gracious to me, God, be gracious to me,
   for I take refuge in you.
   I will seek refuge in the shadow of your wings
   until danger passes.
² I call to God Most High,
   to God who fulfills his purpose for me.
³ He reaches down from heaven and saves me,
   challenging the one who tramples me.   Selah
   God sends his faithful love and truth.
⁴ I am surrounded by lions;
   I lie down among devouring lions—
   people whose teeth are spears and arrows,
   whose tongues are sharp swords.
⁵ God, be exalted above the heavens;
   let your glory be over the whole earth.
⁶ They prepared a net for my steps;
   I was despondent.
   They dug a pit ahead of me,
   but they fell into it!   Selah

⁷ My heart is confident, God, my heart is confident.
   I will sing; I will sing praises.
⁸ Wake up, my soul!
   Wake up, harp and lyre!
   I will wake up the dawn.
⁹ I will praise you, Lord, among the peoples;
   I will sing praises to you among the nations.
¹⁰ For your faithful love is as high as the heavens;
   your faithfulness reaches the clouds.
¹¹ God, be exalted above the heavens;
   let your glory be over the whole earth.

Consider where your focus is today. Is it on your troubles? Look above them. Put God above your storms and remind your soul who God is and whose you are.

PSALM 58
A Cry against Injustice
For the choir director: "Do Not Destroy." A Miktam of David.

1 Do you really speak righteously, you mighty ones?
Do you judge people fairly?
2 No, you practice injustice in your hearts;
with your hands you weigh out violence in the land.

3 The wicked go astray from the womb;
liars wander about from birth.
4 They have venom like the venom of a snake,
like the deaf cobra that stops up its ears,
5 that does not listen to the sound of the charmers
who skillfully weave spells.

6 God, knock the teeth out of their mouths;
LORD, tear out the young lions' fangs.
7 May they vanish like water that flows by;
may they aim their blunted arrows.
8 Like a slug that moves along in slime,
like a woman's miscarried child,
may they not see the sun.

9 Before your pots can feel the heat of the thorns—
whether green or burning—
he will sweep them away.
10 The righteous one will rejoice
when he sees the retribution;
he will wash his feet in the blood of the wicked.
11 Then people will say,
"Yes, there is a reward for the righteous!
There is a God who judges on earth!"

PSALM 59
God Our Stronghold
For the choir director: "Do Not Destroy." A Miktam of David. When Saul sent agents to watch the house and kill him.

1 Rescue me from my enemies, my God;
protect me from those who rise up against me.
2 Rescue me from those who practice sin,
and save me from men of bloodshed.
3 Because look, LORD, they set an ambush for me.
Powerful men attack me,
but not because of any sin or rebellion of mine.
4 For no fault of mine,
they run and take up a position.
Awake to help me, and take notice.
5 LORD God of Armies, you are the God of Israel.
Rise up to punish all the nations;
do not show favor to any wicked traitors.   *Selah*

When the wicked prosper, the vulnerable suffer. What injustice burdens your heart today? Join the prayers of the saints.

News reports can unnerve us. But Jesus strengthens us. Fix your eyes on him. Tell him what he means to you. It will put things in perspective.

⁶ They return at evening, snarling like dogs
and prowling around the city.
⁷ Look, they spew from their mouths—
sharp words from their lips.
"For who," they say, "will hear?"
⁸ But you laugh at them, LORD;
you ridicule all the nations.
⁹ I will keep watch for you, my strength,
because God is my stronghold.
¹⁰ My faithful God will come to meet me;
God will let me look down on my adversaries.

¹¹ Do not kill them; otherwise, my people will forget.
By your power, make them homeless wanderers
and bring them down,
Lord, our shield.
¹² For the sin of their mouths and the words of their lips,
let them be caught in their pride.
They utter curses and lies.
¹³ Consume them in rage;
consume them until they are gone.
Then people will know throughout the earth
that God rules over Jacob.   *Selah*

¹⁴ And they return at evening, snarling like dogs
and prowling around the city.
¹⁵ They scavenge for food;
they growl if they are not satisfied.

¹⁶ But I will sing of your strength
and will joyfully proclaim
your faithful love in the morning.
For you have been a stronghold for me,
a refuge in my day of trouble.
¹⁷ To you, my strength, I sing praises,
because God is my stronghold—
my faithful God.

PSALM 60
Prayer in Difficult Times

For the choir director: according to "The Lily of Testimony." A Miktam of David for teaching. When he fought with Aram-naharaim and Aram-zobah, and Joab returned and struck Edom in Salt Valley, killing twelve thousand.

¹ God, you have rejected us;
you have broken us down;
you have been angry. Restore us!
² You have shaken the land and split it open.
Heal its fissures, for it shudders.
³ You have made your people suffer hardship;
you have given us wine to drink
that made us stagger.

When God seems distant and silent, remember this: He draws near to those who fear him. Draw humbly near to him.

⁴ You have given a signal flag to those who fear you,
  so that they can flee before the archers.   Selah
⁵ Save with your right hand, and answer me,
  so that those you love may be rescued.

⁶ God has spoken in his sanctuary:
  "I will celebrate!
  I will divide up Shechem.
  I will apportion the Valley of Succoth.
⁷ Gilead is mine, Manasseh is mine,
  and Ephraim is my helmet;
  Judah is my scepter.
⁸ Moab is my washbasin.
  I throw my sandal on Edom;
  I shout in triumph over Philistia."

⁹ Who will bring me to the fortified city?
  Who will lead me to Edom?
¹⁰ God, haven't you rejected us?
  God, you do not march out with our armies.
¹¹ Give us aid against the foe,
  for human help is worthless.
¹² With God we will perform valiantly;
  he will trample our foes.

PSALM 61
Security in God
For the choir director: on stringed instruments. Of David.

¹ God, hear my cry;
  pay attention to my prayer.
² I call to you from the ends of the earth
  when my heart is without strength.
  Lead me to a rock that is high above me,
³ for you have been a refuge for me,
  a strong tower in the face of the enemy.
⁴ I will dwell in your tent forever
  and take refuge under the shelter of your wings.   Selah

⁵ God, you have heard my vows;
  you have given a heritage
  to those who fear your name.
⁶ Add days to the king's life;
  may his years span many generations.
⁷ May he sit enthroned before God forever.
  Appoint faithful love and truth to guard him.
⁸ Then I will continually sing of your name,
  fulfilling my vows day by day.

Do you feel overwhelmed under your circumstances? What is truer than your circumstances? Your heir status. God's promises. His love. Remind your soul today.

PSALM 62
Trust in God Alone
For the choir director: according to Jeduthun. A psalm of David.

1. I am at rest in God alone;
 my salvation comes from him.
2. He alone is my rock and my salvation,
 my stronghold; I will never be shaken.

3. How long will you threaten a man?
 Will all of you attack
 as if he were a leaning wall
 or a tottering fence?
4. They only plan to bring him down
 from his high position.
 They take pleasure in lying;
 they bless with their mouths,
 but they curse inwardly. *Selah*

5. Rest in God alone, my soul,
 for my hope comes from him.
6. He alone is my rock and my salvation,
 my stronghold; I will not be shaken.
7. My salvation and glory depend on God, my strong rock.
 My refuge is in God.
8. Trust in him at all times, you people;
 pour out your hearts before him.
 God is our refuge. *Selah*

9. Common people are only a vapor;
 important people, an illusion.
 Together on a scale,
 they weigh less than a vapor.
10. Place no trust in oppression,
 or false hope in robbery.
 If wealth increases,
 don't set your heart on it.

11. God has spoken once;
 I have heard this twice:
 strength belongs to God,
12. and faithful love belongs to you, LORD.
 For you repay each according to his works.

PSALM 63
Praise God Who Satisfies
A psalm of David. When he was in the Wilderness of Judah.

1. God, you are my God; I eagerly seek you.
 I thirst for you;
 my body faints for you
 in a land that is dry, desolate, and without water.

If you have trusted Christ with your eternity, you can trust him with your daily burdens. Roll those burdens onto him today. Wait for the Lord.

Nothing on earth satisfies like even a taste of God's presence. Pause and ask him to make himself known to you today.

² So I gaze on you in the sanctuary
to see your strength and your glory.

³ My lips will glorify you
because your faithful love is better than life.
⁴ So I will bless you as long as I live;
at your name, I will lift up my hands.
⁵ You satisfy me as with rich food;
my mouth will praise you with joyful lips.

⁶ When I think of you as I lie on my bed,
I meditate on you during the night watches
⁷ because you are my helper;
I will rejoice in the shadow of your wings.
⁸ I follow close to you;
your right hand holds on to me.

⁹ But those who intend to destroy my life
will go into the depths of the earth.
¹⁰ They will be given over to the power of the sword;
they will become a meal for jackals.
¹¹ But the king will rejoice in God;
all who swear by him will boast,
for the mouths of liars will be shut.

PSALM 64
Protection from Evildoers
For the choir director. A psalm of David.

¹ God, hear my voice when I am in anguish.
Protect my life from the terror of the enemy.
² Hide me from the scheming of wicked people,
from the mob of evildoers,
³ who sharpen their tongues like swords
and aim bitter words like arrows,
⁴ shooting from concealed places at the blameless.
They shoot at him suddenly and are not afraid.
⁵ They adopt an evil plan;
they talk about hiding traps and say,
"Who will see them?"
⁶ They devise crimes and say,
"We have perfected a secret plan."
The inner man and the heart are mysterious.

⁷ But God will shoot them with arrows;
suddenly, they will be wounded.
⁸ They will be made to stumble;
their own tongues work against them.
All who see them will shake their heads.
⁹ Then everyone will fear
and will tell about God's work,
for they will understand what he has done.

A day of reckoning is coming for the wicked. But in the meantime, we call on the name of the Lord to intervene where the wicked are on the move.

¹⁰ The righteous one rejoices in the LORD
and takes refuge in him;
all those who are upright in heart
will offer praise.

PSALM 65
God's Care for the Earth
For the choir director. A psalm of David. A song.

¹ Praise is rightfully yours,
God, in Zion;
vows to you will be fulfilled.
² All humanity will come to you,
the one who hears prayer.
³ Iniquities overwhelm me;
only you can atone for our rebellions.
⁴ How happy is the one you choose
and bring near to live in your courts!
We will be satisfied with the goodness of your house,
the holiness of your temple.

⁵ You answer us in righteousness,
with awe-inspiring works,
God of our salvation,
the hope of all the ends of the earth
and of the distant seas.
⁶ You establish the mountains by your power;
you are robed with strength.
⁷ You silence the roar of the seas,
the roar of their waves,
and the tumult of the nations.
⁸ Those who live far away are awed by your signs;
you make east and west shout for joy.

⁹ You visit the earth and water it abundantly,
enriching it greatly.
God's stream is filled with water,
for you prepare the earth in this way,
providing people with grain.
¹⁰ You soften it with showers and bless its growth,
soaking its furrows and leveling its ridges.
¹¹ You crown the year with your goodness;
your carts overflow with plenty.
¹² The wilderness pastures overflow,
and the hills are robed with joy.
¹³ The pastures are clothed with flocks
and the valleys covered with grain.
They shout in triumph; indeed, they sing.

The river of God flows powerfully and freely. Where do you see God moving on the earth?

PSALM 66
Praise for God's Mighty Acts
For the choir director. A song. A psalm.

1. Let the whole earth shout joyfully to God!
2. Sing about the glory of his name;
   make his praise glorious.
3. Say to God, "How awe-inspiring are your works!
   Your enemies will cringe before you
   because of your great strength.
4. The whole earth will worship you
   and sing praise to you.
   They will sing praise to your name."   *Selah*

5. Come and see the wonders of God;
   his acts for humanity are awe-inspiring.
6. He turned the sea into dry land,
   and they crossed the river on foot.
   There we rejoiced in him.
7. He rules forever by his might;
   he keeps his eye on the nations.
   The rebellious should not exalt themselves.   *Selah*
8. Bless our God, you peoples;
   let the sound of his praise be heard.
9. He keeps us alive
   and does not allow our feet to slip.

10. For you, God, tested us;
    you refined us as silver is refined.
11. You lured us into a trap;
    you placed burdens on our backs.
12. You let men ride over our heads;
    we went through fire and water,
    but you brought us out to abundance.

13. I will enter your house with burnt offerings;
    I will pay you my vows
14. that my lips promised
    and my mouth spoke during my distress.
15. I will offer you fattened sheep as burnt offerings,
    with the fragrant smoke of rams;
    I will sacrifice bulls with goats.   *Selah*

16. Come and listen, all who fear God,
    and I will tell what he has done for me.
17. I cried out to him with my mouth,
    and praise was on my tongue.
18. If I had been aware of malice in my heart,
    the Lord would not have listened.
19. However, God has listened;
    he has paid attention to the sound of my prayer.

God is on the move! If someone asked you what God has done in you and around you, what would you say? _____

²⁰ Blessed be God!
He has not turned away my prayer
or turned his faithful love from me.

PSALM 67
All Will Praise God
For the choir director: with stringed instruments. A psalm. A song.

¹ May God be gracious to us and bless us;
may he make his face shine upon us   *Selah*
² so that your way may be known on earth,
your salvation among all nations.

³ Let the peoples praise you, God;
let all the peoples praise you.
⁴ Let the nations rejoice and shout for joy,
for you judge the peoples with fairness
and lead the nations on earth.   *Selah*
⁵ Let the peoples praise you, God,
let all the peoples praise you.

⁶ The earth has produced its harvest;
God, our God, blesses us.
⁷ God will bless us,
and all the ends of the earth will fear him.

PSALM 68
God's Majestic Power
For the choir director. A psalm of David. A song.

¹ God arises. His enemies scatter,
and those who hate him flee from his presence.
² As smoke is blown away,
so you blow them away.
As wax melts before the fire,
so the wicked are destroyed before God.
³ But the righteous are glad;
they rejoice before God and celebrate with joy.

⁴ Sing to God! Sing praises to his name.
Exalt him who rides on the clouds—
his name is the LORD—and celebrate before him.
⁵ God in his holy dwelling is
a father of the fatherless
and a champion of widows.
⁶ God provides homes for those who are deserted.
He leads out the prisoners to prosperity,
but the rebellious live in a scorched land.

⁷ God, when you went out before your people,
when you marched through the desert,   *Selah*

Sometimes we need to pull ourselves out of the smaller story and pray about the bigger story God is writing here on earth. Write a prayer of blessing for the nations.

⁸ the earth trembled and the skies poured rain
before God, the God of Sinai,
before God, the God of Israel.
⁹ You, God, showered abundant rain;
you revived your inheritance when it languished.
¹⁰ Your people settled in it;
God, you provided for the poor by your goodness.
¹¹ The Lord gave the command;
a great company of women brought the good news:
¹² "The kings of the armies flee—they flee!"
She who stays at home divides the spoil.
¹³ While you lie among the sheep pens,
the wings of a dove are covered with silver,
and its feathers with glistening gold.
¹⁴ When the Almighty scattered kings in the land,
it snowed on Zalmon.
¹⁵ Mount Bashan is God's towering mountain;
Mount Bashan is a mountain of many peaks.
¹⁶ Why gaze with envy, you mountain peaks,
at the mountain God desired for his abode?
The LORD will dwell there forever!
¹⁷ God's chariots are tens of thousands,
thousands and thousands;
the Lord is among them in the sanctuary
as he was at Sinai.
¹⁸ You ascended to the heights, taking away captives;
you received gifts from people,
even from the rebellious,
so that the LORD God might dwell there.

¹⁹ Blessed be the Lord!
Day after day he bears our burdens;
God is our salvation.   *Selah*
²⁰ Our God is a God of salvation,
and escape from death belongs to the LORD my Lord.
²¹ Surely God crushes the heads of his enemies,
the hairy brow of one who goes on in his guilty acts.
²² The Lord said, "I will bring them back from Bashan;
I will bring them back from the depths of the sea
²³ so that your foot may wade in blood
and your dogs' tongues may have their share
from the enemies."
²⁴ People have seen your procession, God,
the procession of my God,
my King, in the sanctuary.
²⁵ Singers lead the way,
with musicians following;
among them are young women
playing tambourines.

Confident hope comes from *knowing* God. Draw near. Get to know him better. He wants to show you great and wondrous things.

²⁶ Bless God in the assemblies;
bless the LORD from the fountain of Israel.
²⁷ There is Benjamin, the youngest, leading them,
the rulers of Judah in their assembly,
the rulers of Zebulun, the rulers of Naphtali.

²⁸ Your God has decreed your strength.
Show your strength, God,
you who have acted on our behalf.
²⁹ Because of your temple at Jerusalem,
kings will bring tribute to you.
³⁰ Rebuke the beast in the reeds,
the herd of bulls with the calves of the peoples.
Trample underfoot those with bars of silver.
Scatter the peoples who take pleasure in war.
³¹ Ambassadors will come from Egypt;
Cush will stretch out its hands to God.

³² Sing to God, you kingdoms of the earth;
sing praise to the Lord,   *Selah*
³³ to him who rides in the ancient, highest heavens.
Look, he thunders with his powerful voice!
³⁴ Ascribe power to God.
His majesty is over Israel,
his power is among the clouds.
³⁵ God, you are awe-inspiring in your sanctuaries.
The God of Israel gives power and strength to his people.
Blessed be God!

PSALM 69
A Plea for Rescue
For the choir director: according to "The Lilies." Of David.

¹ Save me, God,
for the water has risen to my neck.
² I have sunk in deep mud, and there is no footing;
I have come into deep water,
and a flood sweeps over me.
³ I am weary from my crying;
my throat is parched.
My eyes fail, looking for my God.
⁴ Those who hate me without cause
are more numerous than the hairs of my head;
my deceitful enemies, who would destroy me,
are powerful.
Though I did not steal, I must repay.

⁵ God, you know my foolishness,
and my guilty acts are not hidden from you.

When the Lord disciplines us, the enemy also seeks to diminish us. Can you discern God's voice over the enemy's? What is he saying to you?

⁶ Do not let those who put their hope in you
be disgraced because of me,
Lord GOD of Armies;
do not let those who seek you
be humiliated because of me,
God of Israel.
⁷ For I have endured insults because of you,
and shame has covered my face.
⁸ I have become a stranger to my brothers
and a foreigner to my mother's sons
⁹ because zeal for your house has consumed me,
and the insults of those who insult you
have fallen on me.
¹⁰ I mourned and fasted,
but it brought me insults.
¹¹ I wore sackcloth as my clothing,
and I was a joke to them.
¹² Those who sit at the city gate talk about me,
and drunkards make up songs about me.

¹³ But as for me, LORD,
my prayer to you is for a time of favor.
In your abundant, faithful love, God,
answer me with your sure salvation.
¹⁴ Rescue me from the miry mud; don't let me sink.
Let me be rescued from those who hate me
and from the deep water.
¹⁵ Don't let the floodwaters sweep over me
or the deep swallow me up;
don't let the Pit close its mouth over me.
¹⁶ Answer me, LORD,
for your faithful love is good.
In keeping with your abundant compassion,
turn to me.
¹⁷ Don't hide your face from your servant,
for I am in distress.
Answer me quickly!
¹⁸ Come near to me and redeem me;
ransom me because of my enemies.

¹⁹ You know the insults I endure—
my shame and disgrace.
You are aware of all my adversaries.
²⁰ Insults have broken my heart,
and I am in despair.
I waited for sympathy,
but there was none;
for comforters, but found no one.
²¹ Instead, they gave me gall for my food,
and for my thirst
they gave me vinegar to drink.

²² Let their table set before them be a snare,
   and let it be a trap for their allies.
²³ Let their eyes grow too dim to see,
   and let their hips continually quake.
²⁴ Pour out your rage on them,
   and let your burning anger overtake them.
²⁵ Make their fortification desolate;
   may no one live in their tents.
²⁶ For they persecute the one you struck
   and talk about the pain of those you wounded.
²⁷ Charge them with crime on top of crime;
   do not let them share in your righteousness.
²⁸ Let them be erased from the book of life
   and not be recorded with the righteous.

²⁹ But as for me—poor and in pain—
   let your salvation protect me, God.
³⁰ I will praise God's name with song
   and exalt him with thanksgiving.
³¹ That will please the LORD more than an ox,
   more than a bull with horns and hooves.
³² The humble will see it and rejoice.
   You who seek God, take heart!
³³ For the LORD listens to the needy
   and does not despise
   his own who are prisoners.

³⁴ Let heaven and earth praise him,
   the seas and everything that moves in them,
³⁵ for God will save Zion
   and build up the cities of Judah.
   They will live there and possess it.
³⁶ The descendants of his servants will inherit it,
   and those who love his name will live in it.

PSALM 70
A Call for Deliverance
For the choir director. Of David. To bring remembrance.

¹ God, hurry to rescue me.
  LORD, hurry to help me!

² Let those who seek to kill me
  be disgraced and confounded;
  let those who wish me harm
  be turned back and humiliated.
³ Let those who say, "Aha, aha!"
  retreat because of their shame.

⁴ Let all who seek you rejoice and be glad in you;
  let those who love your salvation
  continually say, "God is great!"

What is your most urgent need at the moment? Pour out your heart today. God is with you.

⁵ I am oppressed and needy;
  hurry to me, God.
  You are my help and my deliverer;
  LORD, do not delay.

PSALM 71
God's Help in Old Age

¹ LORD, I seek refuge in you;
  let me never be disgraced.
² In your justice, rescue and deliver me;
  listen closely to me and save me.
³ Be a rock of refuge for me,
  where I can always go.
  Give the command to save me,
  for you are my rock and fortress.
⁴ Deliver me, my God, from the power of the wicked,
  from the grasp of the unjust and oppressive.
⁵ For you are my hope, Lord GOD,
  my confidence from my youth.
⁶ I have leaned on you from birth;
  you took me from my mother's womb.
  My praise is always about you.
⁷ I am like a miraculous sign to many,
  and you are my strong refuge.
⁸ My mouth is full of praise
  and honor to you all day long.

⁹ Don't discard me in my old age.
  As my strength fails, do not abandon me.
¹⁰ For my enemies talk about me,
  and those who spy on me plot together,
¹¹ saying, "God has abandoned him;
  chase him and catch him,
  for there is no one to rescue him."
¹² God, do not be far from me;
  my God, hurry to help me.
¹³ May my adversaries be disgraced and destroyed;
  may those who intend to harm me
  be covered with disgrace and humiliation.
¹⁴ But I will hope continually
  and will praise you more and more.
¹⁵ My mouth will tell about your righteousness
  and your salvation all day long,
  though I cannot sum them up.
¹⁶ I come because of the mighty acts of the Lord GOD;
  I will proclaim your righteousness, yours alone.

¹⁷ God, you have taught me from my youth,
  and I still proclaim your wondrous works.

What message do you have for future generations? _____

¹⁸ Even while I am old and gray,
   God, do not abandon me,
   while I proclaim your power
   to another generation,
   your strength to all who are to come.
¹⁹ Your righteousness reaches the heights, God,
   you who have done great things;
   God, who is like you?
²⁰ You caused me to experience
   many troubles and misfortunes,
   but you will revive me again.
   You will bring me up again,
   even from the depths of the earth.
²¹ You will increase my honor
   and comfort me once again.
²² Therefore, I will praise you with a harp
   for your faithfulness, my God;
   I will sing to you with a lyre,
   Holy One of Israel.
²³ My lips will shout for joy
   when I sing praise to you
   because you have redeemed me.
²⁴ Therefore, my tongue will proclaim
   your righteousness all day long,
   for those who intend to harm me
   will be disgraced and confounded.

PSALM 72
A Prayer for the King
Of Solomon.

¹ God, give your justice to the king
   and your righteousness to the king's son.
² He will judge your people with righteousness
   and your afflicted ones with justice.
³ May the mountains bring well-being to the people
   and the hills, righteousness.
⁴ May he vindicate the afflicted among the people,
   help the poor,
   and crush the oppressor.
⁵ May they fear you while the sun endures
   and as long as the moon, throughout all generations.
⁶ May the king be like rain that falls on the cut grass,
   like spring showers that water the earth.
⁷ May the righteous flourish in his days
   and well-being abound
   until the moon is no more.
⁸ May he rule from sea to sea
   and from the Euphrates
   to the ends of the earth.

We all have a sphere of influence. Pray that others might flourish because of the ways God has gifted and called *you*.

⁹ May desert tribes kneel before him
and his enemies lick the dust.
¹⁰ May the kings of Tarshish
and the coasts and islands bring tribute,
the kings of Sheba and Seba offer gifts.
¹¹ Let all kings bow in homage to him,
all nations serve him.

¹² For he will rescue the poor who cry out
and the afflicted who have no helper.
¹³ He will have pity on the poor and helpless
and save the lives of the poor.
¹⁴ He will redeem them from oppression and violence,
for their lives are precious in his sight.

¹⁵ May he live long!
May gold from Sheba be given to him.
May prayer be offered for him continually,
and may he be blessed all day long.
¹⁶ May there be plenty of grain in the land;
may it wave on the tops of the mountains.
May its crops be like Lebanon.
May people flourish in the cities
like the grass of the field.
¹⁷ May his name endure forever;
as long as the sun shines,
may his fame increase.
May all nations be blessed by him
and call him blessed.

¹⁸ Blessed be the LORD God, the God of Israel,
who alone does wonders.
¹⁹ Blessed be his glorious name forever;
the whole earth is filled with his glory.
Amen and amen.
²⁰ The prayers of David son of Jesse are concluded.

PSALM 73
God's Ways Vindicated
A psalm of Asaph.

¹ God is indeed good to Israel,
to the pure in heart.
² But as for me, my feet almost slipped;
my steps nearly went astray.
³ For I envied the arrogant;
I saw the prosperity of the wicked.

⁴ They have an easy time until they die,
and their bodies are well fed.
⁵ They are not in trouble like others;
they are not afflicted like most people.

Whatever troubles you, remember that nothing can separate you from God's love. He's got you. He won't let go. And he will guide you safely home. Remind your soul today.

⁶ Therefore, pride is their necklace,
  and violence covers them like a garment.
⁷ Their eyes bulge out from fatness;
  the imaginations of their hearts run wild.
⁸ They mock, and they speak maliciously;
  they arrogantly threaten oppression.
⁹ They set their mouths against heaven,
  and their tongues strut across the earth.
¹⁰ Therefore his people turn to them
  and drink in their overflowing words.
¹¹ The wicked say, "How can God know?
  Does the Most High know everything?"
¹² Look at them—the wicked!
  They are always at ease,
  and they increase their wealth.

¹³ Did I purify my heart
  and wash my hands in innocence for nothing?
¹⁴ For I am afflicted all day long
  and punished every morning.
¹⁵ If I had decided to say these things aloud,
  I would have betrayed your people.
¹⁶ When I tried to understand all this,
  it seemed hopeless
¹⁷ until I entered God's sanctuary.
  Then I understood their destiny.
¹⁸ Indeed, you put them in slippery places;
  you make them fall into ruin.
¹⁹ How suddenly they become a desolation!
  They come to an end, swept away by terrors.
²⁰ Like one waking from a dream,
  Lord, when arising, you will despise their image.

²¹ When I became embittered
  and my innermost being was wounded,
²² I was stupid and didn't understand;
  I was an unthinking animal toward you.
²³ Yet I am always with you;
  you hold my right hand.
²⁴ You guide me with your counsel,
  and afterward you will take me up in glory.
²⁵ Who do I have in heaven but you?
  And I desire nothing on earth but you.
²⁶ My flesh and my heart may fail,
  but God is the strength of my heart,
  my portion forever.
²⁷ Those far from you will certainly perish;
  you destroy all who are unfaithful to you.
²⁸ But as for me, God's presence is my good.
  I have made the Lord GOD my refuge,
  so I can tell about all you do.

PSALM 74
Prayer for Israel
A Maskil of Asaph.

1. Why have you rejected us forever, God?
Why does your anger burn
against the sheep of your pasture?
2. Remember your congregation,
which you purchased long ago
and redeemed as the tribe for your own possession.
Remember Mount Zion where you dwell.
3. Make your way to the perpetual ruins,
to all that the enemy has destroyed in the sanctuary.
4. Your adversaries roared in the meeting place
where you met with us.
They set up their emblems as signs.
5. It was like men in a thicket of trees,
wielding axes,
6. then smashing all the carvings
with hatchets and picks.
7. They set your sanctuary on fire;
they utterly desecrated
the dwelling place of your name.
8. They said in their hearts,
"Let us oppress them relentlessly."
They burned every place throughout the land
where God met with us.
9. There are no signs for us to see.
There is no longer a prophet.
And none of us knows how long this will last.
10. God, how long will the enemy mock?
Will the foe insult your name forever?
11. Why do you hold back your hand?
Stretch out your right hand and destroy them!

12. God my King is from ancient times,
performing saving acts on the earth.
13. You divided the sea with your strength;
you smashed the heads of the sea monsters in the water;
14. you crushed the heads of Leviathan;
you fed him to the creatures of the desert.
15. You opened up springs and streams;
you dried up ever-flowing rivers.
16. The day is yours, also the night;
you established the moon and the sun.
17. You set all the boundaries of the earth;
you made summer and winter.

18. Remember this: the enemy has mocked the LORD,
and a foolish people has insulted your name.

God is stronger than the fiercest enemy. Ask him to foil the plans of the wicked and establish the plans of the righteous. Pray the Lord's promises.

¹⁹ Do not give to beasts the life of your dove;
  do not forget the lives of your poor people forever.
²⁰ Consider the covenant,
  for the dark places of the land are full of violence.
²¹ Do not let the oppressed turn away in shame;
  let the poor and needy praise your name.
²² Rise up, God, champion your cause!
  Remember the insults
  that fools bring against you all day long.
²³ Do not forget the clamor of your adversaries,
  the tumult of your opponents that goes up constantly.

PSALM 75
God Judges the Wicked
For the choir director: "Do Not Destroy." A psalm of Asaph. A song.

¹ We give thanks to you, God;
  we give thanks to you, for your name is near.
  People tell about your wondrous works.

² "When I choose a time,
  I will judge fairly.
³ When the earth and all its inhabitants shake,
  I am the one who steadies its pillars.   Selah
⁴ I say to the boastful, 'Do not boast,'
  and to the wicked, 'Do not lift up your horn.
⁵ Do not lift up your horn against heaven
  or speak arrogantly.' "

⁶ Exaltation does not come
  from the east, the west, or the desert,
⁷ for God is the Judge:
  He brings down one and exalts another.
⁸ For there is a cup in the LORD's hand,
  full of wine blended with spices, and he pours from it.
  All the wicked of the earth will drink,
  draining it to the dregs.
⁹ As for me, I will tell about him forever;
  I will sing praise to the God of Jacob.

¹⁰ "I will cut off all the horns of the wicked,
  but the horns of the righteous will be lifted up."

PSALM 76
God, the Powerful Judge
For the choir director: with stringed instruments. A psalm of Asaph. A song.

¹ God is known in Judah;
  his name is great in Israel.
² His tent is in Salem,
  his dwelling place in Zion.

God promises to cut off the strength of the wicked and to increase the power of the godly. Imagine that shift of power taking place on the earth! Pray in faith. _____

We are on the winning side of the battle. Who can stand against the Lord? Pay God tribute today. _____

3 There he shatters the bow's flaming arrows,
   the shield, the sword, and the weapons of war.   Selah

4 You are resplendent and majestic
   coming down from the mountains of prey.
5 The brave-hearted have been plundered;
   they have slipped into their final sleep.
   None of the warriors was able to lift a hand.
6 At your rebuke, God of Jacob,
   both chariot and horse lay still.

7 And you—you are to be feared.
   When you are angry,
   who can stand before you?
8 From heaven you pronounced judgment.
   The earth feared and grew quiet
9 when God rose up to judge
   and to save all the lowly of the earth.   Selah
10 Even human wrath will praise you;
    you will clothe yourself
    with the wrath that remains.

11 Make and keep your vows
    to the LORD your God;
    let all who are around him bring tribute
    to the awe-inspiring one.
12 He humbles the spirit of leaders;
    he is feared by the kings of the earth.

PSALM 77
Confidence in a Time of Crisis
*For the choir director: according to Jeduthun.
Of Asaph. A psalm.*

1 I cry aloud to God,
   aloud to God, and he will hear me.
2 I sought the Lord in my day of trouble.
   My hands were continually lifted up
   all night long;
   I refused to be comforted.
3 I think of God; I groan;
   I meditate; my spirit becomes weak.   Selah

4 You have kept me from closing my eyes;
   I am troubled and cannot speak.
5 I consider days of old,
   years long past.
6 At night I remember my music;
   I meditate in my heart, and my spirit ponders.

7 "Will the Lord reject forever
   and never again show favor?

When God seems silent, remember your history with him. Remember his faithfulness to you. Write it down.

⁸ Has his faithful love ceased forever?
   Is his promise at an end for all generations?
⁹ Has God forgotten to be gracious?
   Has he in anger withheld his compassion?"   Selah

¹⁰ So I say, "I am grieved
    that the right hand of the Most High has changed."
¹¹ I will remember the LORD's works;
    yes, I will remember your ancient wonders.
¹² I will reflect on all you have done
    and meditate on your actions.

¹³ God, your way is holy.
    What god is great like God?
¹⁴ You are the God who works wonders;
    you revealed your strength among the peoples.
¹⁵ With power you redeemed your people,
    the descendants of Jacob and Joseph.   Selah

¹⁶ The water saw you, God.
    The water saw you; it trembled.
    Even the depths shook.
¹⁷ The clouds poured down water.
    The storm clouds thundered;
    your arrows flashed back and forth.
¹⁸ The sound of your thunder was in the whirlwind;
    lightning lit up the world.
    The earth shook and quaked.
¹⁹ Your way went through the sea
    and your path through the vast water,
    but your footprints were unseen.
²⁰ You led your people like a flock
    by the hand of Moses and Aaron.

PSALM 78
Lessons from Israel's Past
A Maskil of Asaph.

¹ My people, hear my instruction;
  listen to the words from my mouth.
² I will declare wise sayings;
  I will speak mysteries from the past—
³ things we have heard and known
  and that our fathers have passed down to us.
⁴ We will not hide them from their children,
  but will tell a future generation
  the praiseworthy acts of the LORD,
  his might, and the wondrous works
  he has performed.
⁵ He established a testimony in Jacob
  and set up a law in Israel,
  which he commanded our fathers
  to teach to their children

If we forget what God has done, we won't anticipate what he might do.

Based on your history with God, what do you know to be true about him?

⁶ so that a future generation—
children yet to be born—might know.
They were to rise and tell their children
⁷ so that they might put their confidence in God
and not forget God's works,
but keep his commands.
⁸ Then they would not be like their fathers,
a stubborn and rebellious generation,
a generation whose heart was not loyal
and whose spirit was not faithful to God.

⁹ The Ephraimite archers turned back
on the day of battle.
¹⁰ They did not keep God's covenant
and refused to live by his law.
¹¹ They forgot what he had done,
the wondrous works he had shown them.
¹² He worked wonders in the sight of their fathers
in the land of Egypt, the territory of Zoan.
¹³ He split the sea and brought them across;
the water stood firm like a wall.
¹⁴ He led them with a cloud by day
and with a fiery light throughout the night.
¹⁵ He split rocks in the wilderness
and gave them drink as abundant as the depths.
¹⁶ He brought streams out of the stone
and made water flow down like rivers.

¹⁷ But they continued to sin against him,
rebelling in the desert against the Most High.
¹⁸ They deliberately tested God,
demanding the food they craved.
¹⁹ They spoke against God, saying,
"Is God able to provide food in the wilderness?
²⁰ Look! He struck the rock and water gushed out;
torrents overflowed.
But can he also provide bread
or furnish meat for his people?"
²¹ Therefore, the LORD heard and became furious;
then fire broke out against Jacob,
and anger flared up against Israel
²² because they did not believe God
or rely on his salvation.
²³ He gave a command to the clouds above
and opened the doors of heaven.
²⁴ He rained manna for them to eat;
he gave them grain from heaven.
²⁵ People ate the bread of angels.
He sent them an abundant supply of food.
²⁶ He made the east wind blow in the skies
and drove the south wind by his might.

²⁷ He rained meat on them like dust,
   and winged birds like the sand of the seas.
²⁸ He made them fall in the camp,
   all around the tents.
²⁹ The people ate and were completely satisfied,
   for he gave them what they craved.
³⁰ Before they had turned from what they craved,
   while the food was still in their mouths,
³¹ God's anger flared up against them,
   and he killed some of their best men.
   He struck down Israel's fit young men.

³² Despite all this, they kept sinning
   and did not believe his wondrous works.
³³ He made their days end in futility,
   their years in sudden disaster.
³⁴ When he killed some of them,
   the rest began to seek him;
   they repented and searched for God.
³⁵ They remembered that God was their rock,
   the Most High God, their Redeemer.
³⁶ But they deceived him with their mouths,
   they lied to him with their tongues,
³⁷ their hearts were insincere toward him,
   and they were unfaithful to his covenant.
³⁸ Yet he was compassionate;
   he atoned for their iniquity
   and did not destroy them.
   He often turned his anger aside
   and did not unleash all his wrath.
³⁹ He remembered that they were only flesh,
   a wind that passes and does not return.

⁴⁰ How often they rebelled against him
   in the wilderness
   and grieved him in the desert.
⁴¹ They constantly tested God
   and provoked the Holy One of Israel.
⁴² They did not remember his power shown
   on the day he redeemed them from the foe,
⁴³ when he performed his miraculous signs in Egypt
   and his wonders in the territory of Zoan.
⁴⁴ He turned their rivers into blood,
   and they could not drink from their streams.
⁴⁵ He sent among them swarms of flies,
   which fed on them,
   and frogs, which devastated them.
⁴⁶ He gave their crops to the caterpillar
   and the fruit of their labor to the locust.
⁴⁷ He killed their vines with hail
   and their sycamore fig trees with a flood.

⁴⁸ He handed over their livestock to hail
  and their cattle to lightning bolts.
⁴⁹ He sent his burning anger against them:
  fury, indignation, and calamity—
  a band of deadly messengers.
⁵⁰ He cleared a path for his anger.
  He did not spare them from death
  but delivered their lives to the plague.
⁵¹ He struck all the firstborn in Egypt,
  the first progeny of the tents of Ham.
⁵² He led his people out like sheep
  and guided them like a flock in the wilderness.
⁵³ He led them safely, and they were not afraid;
  but the sea covered their enemies.
⁵⁴ He brought them to his holy territory,
  to the mountain his right hand acquired.
⁵⁵ He drove out nations before them.
  He apportioned their inheritance by lot
  and settled the tribes of Israel in their tents.

⁵⁶ But they rebelliously tested the Most High God,
  for they did not keep his decrees.
⁵⁷ They treacherously turned away like their fathers;
  they became warped like a faulty bow.
⁵⁸ They enraged him with their high places
  and provoked his jealousy with their carved images.
⁵⁹ God heard and became furious;
  he completely rejected Israel.
⁶⁰ He abandoned the tabernacle at Shiloh,
  the tent where he resided among mankind.
⁶¹ He gave up his strength to captivity
  and his splendor to the hand of a foe.
⁶² He surrendered his people to the sword
  because he was enraged with his heritage.
⁶³ Fire consumed his chosen young men,
  and his young women had no wedding songs.
⁶⁴ His priests fell by the sword,
  and the widows could not lament.

⁶⁵ The Lord awoke as if from sleep,
  like a warrior from the effects of wine.
⁶⁶ He beat back his foes;
  he gave them lasting disgrace.
⁶⁷ He rejected the tent of Joseph
  and did not choose the tribe of Ephraim.
⁶⁸ He chose instead the tribe of Judah,
  Mount Zion, which he loved.
⁶⁹ He built his sanctuary like the heights,
  like the earth that he established forever.
⁷⁰ He chose David his servant
  and took him from the sheep pens;

⁷¹ he brought him from tending ewes
to be shepherd over his people Jacob—
over Israel, his inheritance.
⁷² He shepherded them with a pure heart
and guided them with his skillful hands.

PSALM 79
Faith amid Confusion
A psalm of Asaph.

¹ God, the nations have invaded your inheritance,
desecrated your holy temple,
and turned Jerusalem into ruins.
² They gave the corpses of your servants
to the birds of the sky for food,
the flesh of your faithful ones
to the beasts of the earth.
³ They poured out their blood
like water all around Jerusalem,
and there was no one to bury them.
⁴ We have become an object of reproach
to our neighbors,
a source of mockery and ridicule
to those around us.

⁵ How long, LORD? Will you be angry forever?
Will your jealousy keep burning like fire?
⁶ Pour out your wrath on the nations
that don't acknowledge you,
on the kingdoms that don't call on your name,
⁷ for they have devoured Jacob
and devastated his homeland.
⁸ Do not hold past iniquities against us;
let your compassion come to us quickly,
for we have become very weak.

⁹ God of our salvation, help us—
for the glory of your name.
Rescue us and atone for our sins,
for your name's sake.
¹⁰ Why should the nations ask,
"Where is their God?"
Before our eyes,
let vengeance for the shed blood of your servants
be known among the nations.
¹¹ Let the groans of the prisoners reach you;
according to your great power,
preserve those condemned to die.
¹² Pay back sevenfold to our neighbors
the reproach they have hurled at you, Lord.

Pray for your nation based on God's goodness, not on man's badness. Ask Jesus to intervene and heal and move in supernatural ways.

¹³ Then we, your people, the sheep of your pasture,
    will thank you forever;
    we will declare your praise
    to generation after generation.

PSALM 80
A Prayer for Restoration
For the choir director: according to "The Lilies." A testimony of Asaph. A psalm.

¹ Listen, Shepherd of Israel,
    who leads Joseph like a flock;
    you who sit enthroned between the cherubim,
    shine ² on Ephraim,
    Benjamin, and Manasseh.
    Rally your power and come to save us.
³ Restore us, God;
    make your face shine on us,
    so that we may be saved.

⁴ LORD God of Armies,
    how long will you be angry
    with your people's prayers?
⁵ You fed them the bread of tears
    and gave them a full measure
    of tears to drink.
⁶ You put us at odds with our neighbors;
    our enemies mock us.
⁷ Restore us, God of Armies;
    make your face shine on us, so that we may be saved.

⁸ You dug up a vine from Egypt;
    you drove out the nations and planted it.
⁹ You cleared a place for it;
    it took root and filled the land.
¹⁰ The mountains were covered by its shade,
    and the mighty cedars with its branches.
¹¹ It sent out sprouts toward the Sea
    and shoots toward the River.
¹² Why have you broken down its walls
    so that all who pass by pick its fruit?
¹³ Boars from the forest tear at it
    and creatures of the field feed on it.
¹⁴ Return, God of Armies.
    Look down from heaven and see;
    take care of this vine,
¹⁵ the root your right hand planted,
    the son that you made strong for yourself.
¹⁶ It was cut down and burned;
    they perish at the rebuke of your countenance.

It takes courage and humility to pray "we" and "us" prayers on behalf of your fellow citizens. But that is what intercessors and saints do. Stand in the gap for your nation today.

¹⁷ Let your hand be with the man at your right hand,
with the son of man
you have made strong for yourself.
¹⁸ Then we will not turn away from you;
revive us, and we will call on your name.
¹⁹ Restore us, LORD, the God of Armies;
make your face shine on us, so that we may be saved.

PSALM 81
A Call to Obedience
For the choir director: on the Gittith. Of Asaph.

¹ Sing for joy to God our strength;
shout in triumph to the God of Jacob.
² Lift up a song—play the tambourine,
the melodious lyre, and the harp.
³ Blow the horn on the day of our feasts
during the new moon
and during the full moon.
⁴ For this is a statute for Israel,
an ordinance of the God of Jacob.
⁵ He set it up as a decree for Joseph
when he went throughout the land of Egypt.

I heard an unfamiliar language:
⁶ "I relieved his shoulder from the burden;
his hands were freed from carrying the basket.
⁷ You called out in distress, and I rescued you;
I answered you from the thundercloud.
I tested you at the Waters of Meribah.   Selah
⁸ Listen, my people, and I will admonish you.
Israel, if you would only listen to me!
⁹ There must not be a strange god among you;
you must not bow down to a foreign god.
¹⁰ I am the LORD your God,
who brought you up from the land of Egypt.
Open your mouth wide, and I will fill it.
¹¹ "But my people did not listen to my voice;
Israel did not obey me.
¹² So I gave them over to their stubborn hearts
to follow their own plans.
¹³ If only my people would listen to me
and Israel would follow my ways,
¹⁴ I would quickly subdue their enemies
and turn my hand against their foes."
¹⁵ Those who hate the LORD
would cower to him;
their doom would last forever.
¹⁶ But he would feed Israel with the best wheat.
"I would satisfy you with honey from the rock."

Pray that the hard-hearted and the stubborn will become tender and teachable before the Lord.

PSALM 82
A Plea for Righteous Judgment
A psalm of Asaph.

1. God stands in the divine assembly;
   he pronounces judgment among the gods:
2. "How long will you judge unjustly
   and show partiality to the wicked?   *Selah*
3. Provide justice for the needy and the fatherless;
   uphold the rights of the oppressed and the destitute.
4. Rescue the poor and needy;
   save them from the power of the wicked."

5. They do not know or understand;
   they wander in darkness.
   All the foundations of the earth are shaken.

6. I said, "You are gods;
   you are all sons of the Most High.
7. However, you will die like humans
   and fall like any other ruler."

8. Rise up, God, judge the earth,
   for all the nations belong to you.

PSALM 83
Prayer against Enemies
A song. A psalm of Asaph.

1. God, do not keep silent.
   Do not be deaf, God; do not be quiet.
2. See how your enemies make an uproar;
   those who hate you have acted arrogantly.
3. They devise clever schemes against your people;
   they conspire against your treasured ones.
4. They say, "Come, let us wipe them out as a nation
   so that Israel's name will no longer be remembered."
5. For they have conspired with one mind;
   they form an alliance against you—
6. the tents of Edom and the Ishmaelites,
   Moab and the Hagrites,
7. Gebal, Ammon, and Amalek,
   Philistia with the inhabitants of Tyre.
8. Even Assyria has joined them;
   they lend support to the sons of Lot.   *Selah*

9. Deal with them as you did with Midian,
   as you did with Sisera
   and Jabin at the Kishon River.
10. They were destroyed at En-dor;
    they became manure for the ground.

May God hear your prayer today on behalf of the slave, the poor, the orphan, the refugee, and the victim of human trafficking. In due time, God *will* rise up in response to our prayers!

May people throughout the world awaken to the truth that there is no one like the Lord God Almighty. May your prayers change the world.

¹¹ Make their nobles like Oreb and Zeeb,
and all their tribal leaders like Zebah and Zalmunna,
¹² who said, "Let us seize God's pastures for ourselves."

¹³ Make them like tumbleweed, my God,
like straw before the wind.
¹⁴ As fire burns a forest,
as a flame blazes through mountains,
¹⁵ so pursue them with your tempest
and terrify them with your storm.
¹⁶ Cover their faces with shame
so that they will seek your name LORD.
¹⁷ Let them be put to shame and terrified forever;
let them perish in disgrace.
¹⁸ May they know that you alone—
whose name is the LORD—
are the Most High over the whole earth.

PSALM 84
Longing for God's House

For the choir director: on the Gittith. A psalm of the sons of Korah.

¹ How lovely is your dwelling place,
LORD of Armies.
² I long and yearn
for the courts of the LORD;
my heart and flesh cry out for the living God.

³ Even a sparrow finds a home,
and a swallow, a nest for herself
where she places her young—
near your altars, LORD of Armies,
my King and my God.
⁴ How happy are those who reside in your house,
who praise you continually. *Selah*

⁵ Happy are the people whose strength is in you,
whose hearts are set on pilgrimage.
⁶ As they pass through the Valley of Baca,
they make it a source of springwater;
even the autumn rain will cover it with blessings.
⁷ They go from strength to strength;
each appears before God in Zion.

⁸ LORD God of Armies, hear my prayer;
listen, God of Jacob. *Selah*
⁹ Consider our shield, God;
look on the face of your anointed one.

¹⁰ Better a day in your courts
than a thousand anywhere else.
I would rather stand at the threshold of the house of my God
than live in the tents of wicked people.

God's presence is better than our heart's desires. Even so, he gives good gifts to his children when the time is right. Draw near and trust his timing today.

11 For the LORD God is a sun and shield.
   The LORD grants favor and honor;
   he does not withhold the good
   from those who live with integrity.
12 Happy is the person who trusts in you,
   LORD of Armies!

PSALM 85
Restoration of Favor
For the choir director. A psalm of the sons of Korah.

1 LORD, you showed favor to your land;
  you restored the fortunes of Jacob.
2 You forgave your people's guilt;
  you covered all their sin. *Selah*
3 You withdrew all your fury;
  you turned from your burning anger.

4 Return to us, God of our salvation,
  and abandon your displeasure with us.
5 Will you be angry with us forever?
  Will you prolong your anger for all generations?
6 Will you not revive us again
  so that your people may rejoice in you?
7 Show us your faithful love, LORD,
  and give us your salvation.

8 I will listen to what God will say;
  surely the LORD will declare peace
  to his people, his faithful ones,
  and not let them go back to foolish ways.
9 His salvation is very near those who fear him,
  so that glory may dwell in our land.

10 Faithful love and truth will join together;
   righteousness and peace will embrace.
11 Truth will spring up from the earth,
   and righteousness will look down from heaven.
12 Also, the LORD will provide what is good,
   and our land will yield its crops.
13 Righteousness will go before him
   to prepare the way for his steps.

PSALM 86
Lament and Petition
A prayer of David.

1 Listen, LORD, and answer me,
  for I am poor and needy.
2 Protect my life, for I am faithful.
  You are my God; save your servant who trusts in you.

Your personal reverence before God has national implications. May you experience a personal revival and may Jesus heal your land. Come humbly before him today. _____

_____

_____

_____

_____

_____

_____

God is kind, compassionate, forgiving, and powerful. He listens when you pray. Tell him what you need today. _____

_____

_____

_____

_____

_____

_____

_____

³ Be gracious to me, Lord,
for I call to you all day long.
⁴ Bring joy to your servant's life,
because I appeal to you, Lord.

⁵ For you, Lord, are kind and ready to forgive,
abounding in faithful love to all who call on you.
⁶ LORD, hear my prayer;
listen to my plea for mercy.
⁷ I call on you in the day of my distress,
for you will answer me.

⁸ Lord, there is no one like you among the gods,
and there are no works like yours.
⁹ All the nations you have made
will come and bow down before you, Lord,
and will honor your name.
¹⁰ For you are great and perform wonders;
you alone are God.

¹¹ Teach me your way, LORD,
and I will live by your truth.
Give me an undivided mind to fear your name.
¹² I will praise you with all my heart, Lord my God,
and will honor your name forever.
¹³ For your faithful love for me is great,
and you rescue my life from the depths of Sheol.

¹⁴ God, arrogant people have attacked me;
a gang of ruthless men intends to kill me.
They do not let you guide them.
¹⁵ But you, Lord, are a compassionate and gracious God,
slow to anger and abounding in faithful love and truth.
¹⁶ Turn to me and be gracious to me.
Give your strength to your servant;
save the son of your female servant.
¹⁷ Show me a sign of your goodness;
my enemies will see and be put to shame
because you, LORD, have helped and comforted me.

PSALM 87
Zion, the City of God
A psalm of the sons of Korah. A song.

¹ The city he founded is on the holy mountains.
² The LORD loves Zion's city gates
more than all the dwellings of Jacob.
³ Glorious things are said about you,
city of God.   *Selah*

⁴ "I will make a record of those who know me:
Rahab, Babylon, Philistia, Tyre, and Cush—
each one was born there."

In Christ, you are a citizen of God's kingdom. You will rule and reign with him! Rejoice in the Lord today.

⁵ And it will be said of Zion,
   "This one and that one were born in her."
   The Most High himself will establish her.
⁶ When he registers the peoples,
   the LORD will record,
   "This one was born there."   *Selah*
⁷ Singers and dancers alike will say,
   "My whole source of joy is in you."

PSALM 88
A Cry of Desperation

A song. A psalm of the sons of Korah. For the choir director: according to Mahalath Leannoth. *A Maskil of* Heman the Ezrahite.

¹ LORD, God of my salvation,
   I cry out before you day and night.
² May my prayer reach your presence;
   listen to my cry.
³ For I have had enough troubles,
   and my life is near Sheol.
⁴ I am counted among those going down to the Pit.
   I am like a man without strength,
⁵ abandoned among the dead.
   I am like the slain lying in the grave,
   whom you no longer remember,
   and who are cut off from your care.
⁶ You have put me in the lowest part of the Pit,
   in the darkest places, in the depths.
⁷ Your wrath weighs heavily on me;
   you have overwhelmed me with all your waves.   *Selah*
⁸ You have distanced my friends from me;
   you have made me repulsive to them.
   I am shut in and cannot go out.
⁹ My eyes are worn out from crying.
   LORD, I cry out to you all day long;
   I spread out my hands to you.
¹⁰ Do you work wonders for the dead?
   Do departed spirits rise up to praise you?   *Selah*
¹¹ Will your faithful love be declared in the grave,
   your faithfulness in Abaddon?
¹² Will your wonders be known in the darkness
   or your righteousness in the land of oblivion?
¹³ But I call to you for help, LORD;
   in the morning my prayer meets you.
¹⁴ LORD, why do you reject me?
   Why do you hide your face from me?

If you (or someone you love) is desperate for God's merciful intervention, tell him so.

15 From my youth,
 I have been suffering and near death.
 I suffer your horrors; I am desperate.
16 Your wrath sweeps over me;
 your terrors destroy me.
17 They surround me like water all day long;
 they close in on me from every side.
18 You have distanced loved one and neighbor from me;
 darkness is my only friend.

PSALM 89
Perplexity about God's Promises
A Maskil of Ethan the Ezrahite.

1 I will sing about the LORD's faithful love forever;
 I will proclaim your faithfulness to all generations
 with my mouth.
2 For I will declare,
 "Faithful love is built up forever;
 you establish your faithfulness in the heavens."

3 The LORD said,
 "I have made a covenant with my chosen one;
 I have sworn an oath to David my servant:
4 'I will establish your offspring forever
 and build up your throne for all generations.' "   Selah

5 LORD, the heavens praise your wonders—
 your faithfulness also—
 in the assembly of the holy ones.
6 For who in the skies can compare with the LORD?
 Who among the heavenly beings is like the LORD?
7 God is greatly feared in the council of the holy ones,
 more awe-inspiring than all who surround him.
8 LORD God of Armies,
 who is strong like you, LORD?
 Your faithfulness surrounds you.
9 You rule the raging sea;
 when its waves surge, you still them.
10 You crushed Rahab like one who is slain;
 you scattered your enemies with your powerful arm.
11 The heavens are yours; the earth also is yours.
 The world and everything in it—you founded them.
12 North and south—you created them.
 Tabor and Hermon shout for joy at your name.
13 You have a mighty arm;
 your hand is powerful;
 your right hand is lifted high.
14 Righteousness and justice are the foundation
 of your throne;
 faithful love and truth go before you.

God is greater than your problems, mightier than your obstacles. Remind your soul today.

¹⁵ Happy are the people who know the joyful shout;
 LORD, they walk in the light from your face.
¹⁶ They rejoice in your name all day long,
 and they are exalted by your righteousness.
¹⁷ For you are their magnificent strength;
 by your favor our horn is exalted.
¹⁸ Surely our shield belongs to the LORD,
 our king to the Holy One of Israel.

¹⁹ You once spoke in a vision to your faithful ones
 and said: "I have granted help to a warrior;
 I have exalted one chosen from the people.
²⁰ I have found David my servant;
 I have anointed him with my sacred oil.
²¹ My hand will always be with him,
 and my arm will strengthen him.
²² The enemy will not oppress him;
 the wicked will not afflict him.
²³ I will crush his foes before him
 and strike those who hate him.
²⁴ My faithfulness and love will be with him,
 and through my name
 his horn will be exalted.
²⁵ I will extend his power to the sea
 and his right hand to the rivers.
²⁶ He will call to me, 'You are my Father,
 my God, the rock of my salvation.'
²⁷ I will also make him my firstborn,
 greatest of the kings of the earth.
²⁸ I will always preserve my faithful love for him,
 and my covenant with him will endure.
²⁹ I will establish his line forever,
 his throne as long as heaven lasts.
³⁰ If his sons abandon my instruction
 and do not live by my ordinances,
³¹ if they dishonor my statutes
 and do not keep my commands,
³² then I will call their rebellion
 to account with the rod,
 their iniquity with blows.
³³ But I will not withdraw
 my faithful love from him
 or betray my faithfulness.
³⁴ I will not violate my covenant
 or change what my lips have said.
³⁵ Once and for all
 I have sworn an oath by my holiness;
 I will not lie to David.
³⁶ His offspring will continue forever,
 his throne like the sun before me,

³⁷ like the moon, established forever,
a faithful witness in the sky."   *Selah*

³⁸ But you have spurned and rejected him;
you have become enraged with your anointed.

³⁹ You have repudiated the covenant with your servant;
you have completely dishonored his crown.

⁴⁰ You have broken down all his walls;
you have reduced his fortified cities to ruins.

⁴¹ All who pass by plunder him;
he has become an object of ridicule
to his neighbors.

⁴² You have lifted high the right hand of his foes;
you have made all his enemies rejoice.

⁴³ You have also turned back his sharp sword
and have not let him stand in battle.

⁴⁴ You have made his splendor cease
and have overturned his throne.

⁴⁵ You have shortened the days of his youth;
you have covered him with shame.   *Selah*

⁴⁶ How long, LORD? Will you hide forever?
Will your anger keep burning like fire?

⁴⁷ Remember how short my life is.
Have you created everyone for nothing?

⁴⁸ What courageous person can live and never see death?
Who can save himself from the power of Sheol?   *Selah*

⁴⁹ Lord, where are the former acts of your faithful love
that you swore to David in your faithfulness?

⁵⁰ Remember, Lord, the ridicule against your servants—
in my heart I carry abuse from all the peoples—

⁵¹ how your enemies have ridiculed, LORD,
how they have ridiculed every step of your anointed.

⁵² Blessed be the LORD forever.
Amen and amen.

PSALM 90
Eternal God and Mortal Man
A prayer of Moses, the man of God.

¹ Lord, you have been our refuge
in every generation.

² Before the mountains were born,
before you gave birth to the earth and the world,
from eternity to eternity, you are God.

³ You return mankind to the dust,
saying, "Return, descendants of Adam."

⁴ For in your sight a thousand years
are like yesterday that passes by,
like a few hours of the night.

To number our days is to see our moments and our days as a sacred gift from a loving Father. Seek the Lord regarding your schedule, that you may gain a heart of wisdom.

5 You end their lives; they sleep.
　They are like grass that grows in the morning—
6 in the morning it sprouts and grows;
　by evening it withers and dries up.

7 For we are consumed by your anger;
　we are terrified by your wrath.
8 You have set our iniquities before you,
　our secret sins in the light of your presence.
9 For all our days ebb away under your wrath;
　we end our years like a sigh.
10 Our lives last seventy years
　or, if we are strong, eighty years.
　Even the best of them are struggle and sorrow;
　indeed, they pass quickly and we fly away.
11 Who understands the power of your anger?
　Your wrath matches the fear that is due you.
12 Teach us to number our days carefully
　so that we may develop wisdom in our hearts.

13 LORD—how long?
　Turn and have compassion on your servants.
14 Satisfy us in the morning with your faithful love
　so that we may shout with joy and be glad all our days.
15 Make us rejoice for as many days as you have humbled us,
　for as many years as we have seen adversity.
16 Let your work be seen by your servants,
　and your splendor by their children.
17 Let the favor of the Lord our God be on us;
　establish for us the work of our hands—
　establish the work of our hands!

PSALM 91
The Protection of the Most High

1 The one who lives under the protection of the Most High
　dwells in the shadow of the Almighty.

2 I will say concerning the LORD, who is my refuge and my fortress,
　my God in whom I trust:
3 He himself will rescue you from the bird trap,
　from the destructive plague.
4 He will cover you with his feathers;
　you will take refuge under his wings.
　His faithfulness will be a protective shield.
5 You will not fear the terror of the night,
　the arrow that flies by day,
6 the plague that stalks in darkness,
　or the pestilence that ravages at noon.
7 Though a thousand fall at your side
　and ten thousand at your right hand,
　the pestilence will not reach you.

When we dwell with God, we can more easily rest in him. Tuck yourself under his wings today and thank him for his loving protection.

⁸ You will only see it with your eyes
and witness the punishment of the wicked.

⁹ Because you have made the LORD—my refuge,
the Most High—your dwelling place,
¹⁰ no harm will come to you;
no plague will come near your tent.
¹¹ For he will give his angels orders concerning you,
to protect you in all your ways.
¹² They will support you with their hands
so that you will not strike your foot against a stone.
¹³ You will tread on the lion and the cobra;
you will trample the young lion and the serpent.

¹⁴ Because he has his heart set on me,
I will deliver him;
I will protect him because he knows my name.
¹⁵ When he calls out to me, I will answer him;
I will be with him in trouble.
I will rescue him and give him honor.
¹⁶ I will satisfy him with a long life
and show him my salvation.

PSALM 92
God's Love and Faithfulness
A psalm. A song for the Sabbath day.

¹ It is good to give thanks to the LORD,
to sing praise to your name, Most High,
² to declare your faithful love in the morning
and your faithfulness at night,
³ with a ten-stringed harp
and the music of a lyre.

⁴ For you have made me rejoice, LORD,
by what you have done;
I will shout for joy
because of the works of your hands.
⁵ How magnificent are your works, LORD,
how profound your thoughts!
⁶ A stupid person does not know,
a fool does not understand this:
⁷ though the wicked sprout like grass
and all evildoers flourish,
they will be eternally destroyed.
⁸ But you, LORD, are exalted forever.
⁹ For indeed, LORD, your enemies—
indeed, your enemies will perish;
all evildoers will be scattered.
¹⁰ You have lifted up my horn
like that of a wild ox;
I have been anointed with the finest oil.

Though the wicked prosper, their doom is sure. But we as God's people will grow in strength and stature! Embrace this faith perspective today.

¹¹ My eyes look at my enemies;
when evildoers rise against me,
my ears hear them.

¹² The righteous thrive like a palm tree
and grow like a cedar tree in Lebanon.
¹³ Planted in the house of the LORD,
they thrive in the courts of our God.
¹⁴ They will still bear fruit in old age,
healthy and green,
¹⁵ to declare: "The LORD is just;
he is my rock,
and there is no unrighteousness in him."

PSALM 93
God's Eternal Reign

¹ The LORD reigns! He is robed in majesty;
the LORD is robed, enveloped in strength.
The world is firmly established;
it cannot be shaken.
² Your throne has been established
from the beginning;
you are from eternity.
³ The floods have lifted up, LORD,
the floods have lifted up their voice;
the floods lift up their pounding waves.
⁴ Greater than the roar of a huge torrent—
the mighty breakers of the sea—
the LORD on high is majestic.

⁵ LORD, your testimonies are completely reliable;
holiness adorns your house
for all the days to come.

PSALM 94
The Just Judge

¹ LORD, God of vengeance—
God of vengeance, shine!
² Rise up, Judge of the earth;
repay the proud what they deserve.
³ LORD, how long will the wicked—
how long will the wicked celebrate?

⁴ They pour out arrogant words;
all the evildoers boast.
⁵ LORD, they crush your people;
they oppress your heritage.
⁶ They kill the widow and the resident alien
and murder the fatherless.

Things are shaking so that which cannot be shaken can be clearly seen. What is *not* shaking right now? God's love. His promises. His Word. How great is our God?

⁷ They say, "The LORD doesn't see it.
　The God of Jacob doesn't pay attention."

⁸ Pay attention, you stupid people!
　Fools, when will you be wise?
⁹ Can the one who shaped the ear not hear,
　the one who formed the eye not see?
¹⁰ The one who instructs nations,
　the one who teaches mankind knowledge—
　does he not discipline?
¹¹ The LORD knows the thoughts of mankind;
　they are futile.

¹² LORD, how happy is anyone you discipline
　and teach from your law
¹³ to give him relief from troubled times
　until a pit is dug for the wicked.
¹⁴ The LORD will not leave his people
　or abandon his heritage,
¹⁵ for the administration of justice will again be righteous,
　and all the upright in heart will follow it.

¹⁶ Who stands up for me against the wicked?
　Who takes a stand for me against evildoers?
¹⁷ If the LORD had not been my helper,
　I would soon rest in the silence of death.
¹⁸ If I say, "My foot is slipping,"
　your faithful love will support me, LORD.
¹⁹ When I am filled with cares,
　your comfort brings me joy.

²⁰ Can a corrupt throne be your ally,
　a throne that makes evil laws?
²¹ They band together against the life of the righteous
　and condemn the innocent to death.
²² But the LORD is my refuge;
　my God is the rock of my protection.
²³ He will pay them back for their sins
　and destroy them for their evil.
　The LORD our God will destroy them.

PSALM 95
Worship and Warning

¹ Come, let us shout joyfully to the LORD,
　shout triumphantly to the rock of our salvation!
² Let us enter his presence with thanksgiving;
　let us shout triumphantly to him in song.

³ For the LORD is a great God,
　a great King above all gods.

God is your strong fortress. Hide yourself in him today. Pray for the vulnerable, for those who are in the path of the wicked.

God holds the depths of the earth in his hands. He is all-knowing, all-powerful. Listen for his voice today.

⁴ The depths of the earth are in his hand,
 and the mountain peaks are his.
⁵ The sea is his; he made it.
 His hands formed the dry land.

⁶ Come, let us worship and bow down;
 let us kneel before the LORD our Maker.
⁷ For he is our God,
 and we are the people of his pasture,
 the sheep under his care.

Today, if you hear his voice:
⁸ Do not harden your hearts as at Meribah,
 as on that day at Massah in the wilderness
⁹ where your fathers tested me;
 they tried me, though they had seen what I did.
¹⁰ For forty years I was disgusted with that generation;
 I said, "They are a people whose hearts go astray;
 they do not know my ways."
¹¹ So I swore in my anger,
 "They will not enter my rest."

PSALM 96
King of the Earth

¹ Sing a new song to the LORD;
 let the whole earth sing to the LORD.
² Sing to the LORD, bless his name;
 proclaim his salvation from day to day.
³ Declare his glory among the nations,
 his wondrous works among all peoples.

⁴ For the LORD is great and is highly praised;
 he is feared above all gods.
⁵ For all the gods of the peoples are idols,
 but the LORD made the heavens.
⁶ Splendor and majesty are before him;
 strength and beauty are in his sanctuary.

⁷ Ascribe to the LORD, you families of the peoples,
 ascribe to the LORD glory and strength.
⁸ Ascribe to the LORD the glory of his name;
 bring an offering and enter his courts.
⁹ Worship the LORD in the splendor of his holiness;
 let the whole earth tremble before him.

¹⁰ Say among the nations: "The LORD reigns.
 The world is firmly established; it cannot be shaken.
 He judges the peoples fairly."
¹¹ Let the heavens be glad and the earth rejoice;
 let the sea and all that fills it resound.
¹² Let the fields and everything in them celebrate.
 Then all the trees of the forest will shout for joy

We so often envision our fears. But what if we envisioned the victory instead? Ask God to give you a fresh vision for what breakthrough will look like for you.

¹³ before the LORD, for he is coming—
for he is coming to judge the earth.
He will judge the world with righteousness
and the peoples with his faithfulness.

PSALM 97
The Majestic King

1 The LORD reigns! Let the earth rejoice;
let the many coasts and islands be glad.

2 Clouds and total darkness surround him;
righteousness and justice are the foundation of his throne.
3 Fire goes before him
and burns up his foes on every side.
4 His lightning lights up the world;
the earth sees and trembles.
5 The mountains melt like wax
at the presence of the LORD—
at the presence of the Lord of the whole earth.

6 The heavens proclaim his righteousness;
all the peoples see his glory.

7 All who serve carved images,
those who boast in idols, will be put to shame.
All the gods must worship him.

8 Zion hears and is glad,
Judah's villages rejoice
because of your judgments, LORD.
9 For you, LORD,
are the Most High over the whole earth;
you are exalted above all the gods.

10 You who love the LORD, hate evil!
He protects the lives of his faithful ones;
he rescues them from the power of the wicked.
11 Light dawns for the righteous,
gladness for the upright in heart.
12 Be glad in the LORD, you righteous ones,
and give thanks to his holy name.

PSALM 98
Praise the King
A psalm.

1 Sing a new song to the LORD,
for he has performed wonders;
his right hand and holy arm
have won him victory.
2 The LORD has made his victory known;
he has revealed his righteousness
in the sight of the nations.

The earth responds to the presence and the power of the living God! Pause and remember his greatness today.

Sing a new song to the Lord Most High. Where is he at work in your life today?

³ He has remembered his love
and faithfulness to the house of Israel;
all the ends of the earth
have seen our God's victory.
⁴ Let the whole earth shout to the LORD;
be jubilant, shout for joy and sing.
⁵ Sing to the LORD with the lyre,
with the lyre and melodious song.
⁶ With trumpets and the blast of the ram's horn
shout triumphantly
in the presence of the LORD, our King.

⁷ Let the sea and all that fills it,
the world and those who live in it, resound.
⁸ Let the rivers clap their hands;
let the mountains shout together for joy
⁹ before the LORD,
for he is coming to judge the earth.
He will judge the world righteously
and the peoples fairly.

PSALM 99
The King Is Holy

¹ The LORD reigns! Let the peoples tremble.
He is enthroned between the cherubim.
Let the earth quake.
² The LORD is great in Zion;
he is exalted above all the peoples.
³ Let them praise your great
and awe-inspiring name.
He is holy.

⁴ The mighty King loves justice.
You have established fairness;
you have administered justice
and righteousness in Jacob.
⁵ Exalt the LORD our God;
bow in worship at his footstool.
He is holy.

⁶ Moses and Aaron were among his priests;
Samuel also was among those calling on his name.
They called to the LORD and he answered them.
⁷ He spoke to them in a pillar of cloud;
they kept his decrees and the statutes he gave them.
⁸ LORD our God, you answered them.
You were a forgiving God to them,
but an avenger of their sinful actions.

⁹ Exalt the LORD our God;
bow in worship at his holy mountain,
for the LORD our God is holy.

God is more holy than we can comprehend, and we need him more desperately than we can fathom. Honor him and humble yourself today.

PSALM 100
Be Thankful
A psalm of thanksgiving.

1 Let the whole earth shout triumphantly to God!
2 Serve the LORD with gladness;
come before him with joyful songs.
3 Acknowledge that the LORD is God.
He made us, and we are his—
his people, the sheep of his pasture.
4 Enter his gates with thanksgiving
and his courts with praise.
Give thanks to him and bless his name.
5 For the LORD is good, and his faithful love endures forever;
his faithfulness, through all generations.

PSALM 101
A Vow of Integrity
A psalm of David.

1 I will sing of faithful love and justice;
I will sing praise to you, LORD.
2 I will pay attention to the way of integrity.
When will you come to me?
I will live with a heart of integrity in my house.
3 I will not let anything worthless guide me.
I hate the practice of transgression;
it will not cling to me.
4 A devious heart will be far from me;
I will not be involved with evil.
5 I will destroy anyone
who secretly slanders his neighbor;
I cannot tolerate anyone
with haughty eyes or an arrogant heart.
6 My eyes favor the faithful of the land
so that they may sit down with me.
The one who follows the way of integrity
may serve me.
7 No one who acts deceitfully
will live in my palace;
the one who tells lies
will not be retained here to guide me.
8 Every morning I will destroy
all the wicked of the land,
wiping out all evildoers from the LORD's city.

Rise up and thank God! He is good! He is faithful! Thank him today with shouts of joy!

Prayerfully come before the Lord today and ask him, "Is there anything out of order in me today? Anything that needs correcting or redirecting?" Listen for his voice.

PSALM 102
Affliction in Light of Eternity
A prayer of a suffering person who is weak and pours out his lament before the Lord.

1 LORD, hear my prayer;
let my cry for help come before you.
2 Do not hide your face from me in my day of trouble.
Listen closely to me;
answer me quickly when I call.

3 For my days vanish like smoke,
and my bones burn like a furnace.
4 My heart is suffering, withered like grass;
I even forget to eat my food.
5 Because of the sound of my groaning,
my flesh sticks to my bones.
6 I am like an eagle owl,
like a little owl among the ruins.
7 I stay awake;
I am like a solitary bird on a roof.
8 My enemies taunt me all day long;
they ridicule and use my name as a curse.
9 I eat ashes like bread
and mingle my drinks with tears
10 because of your indignation and wrath;
for you have picked me up and thrown me aside.
11 My days are like a lengthening shadow,
and I wither away like grass.

12 But you, LORD, are enthroned forever;
your fame endures to all generations.
13 You will rise up and have compassion on Zion,
for it is time to show favor to her—
the appointed time has come.
14 For your servants take delight in its stones
and favor its dust.

15 Then the nations will fear the name of the LORD,
and all the kings of the earth your glory,
16 for the LORD will rebuild Zion;
he will appear in his glory.
17 He will pay attention to the prayer of the destitute
and will not despise their prayer.

18 This will be written for a later generation,
and a people who have not yet been created will praise the LORD:
19 He looked down from his holy heights—
the LORD gazed out from heaven to earth—
20 to hear a prisoner's groaning,
to set free those condemned to die,
21 so that they might declare
the name of the LORD in Zion
and his praise in Jerusalem,

We thrive only by God's grace and mercy. Appeal to him today based on his goodness, not yours.

²² when peoples and kingdoms are assembled
to serve the LORD.

²³ He has broken my strength in midcourse;
he has shortened my days.
²⁴ I say: "My God, do not take me
in the middle of my life!
Your years continue through all generations.
²⁵ Long ago you established the earth,
and the heavens are the work of your hands.
²⁶ They will perish, but you will endure;
all of them will wear out like clothing.
You will change them like a garment,
and they will pass away.
²⁷ But you are the same,
and your years will never end.
²⁸ Your servants' children will dwell securely,
and their offspring will be established before you."

PSALM 103
The Forgiving God
Of David.

¹ My soul, bless the LORD,
and all that is within me, bless his holy name.
² My soul, bless the LORD,
and do not forget all his benefits.

³ He forgives all your iniquity;
he heals all your diseases.
⁴ He redeems your life from the Pit;
he crowns you with faithful love and compassion.
⁵ He satisfies you with good things;
your youth is renewed like the eagle.

⁶ The LORD executes acts of righteousness
and justice for all the oppressed.
⁷ He revealed his ways to Moses,
his deeds to the people of Israel.
⁸ The LORD is compassionate and gracious,
slow to anger and abounding in faithful love.
⁹ He will not always accuse us
or be angry forever.
¹⁰ He has not dealt with us as our sins deserve
or repaid us according to our iniquities.
¹¹ For as high as the heavens are above the earth,
so great is his faithful love
toward those who fear him.
¹² As far as the east is from the west,
so far has he removed
our transgressions from us.

God restores and redeems! May we never forget the good things he has done for us. What has he done for you?

¹³ As a father has compassion on his children,
   so the LORD has compassion on those who fear him.
¹⁴ For he knows what we are made of,
   remembering that we are dust.

¹⁵ As for man, his days are like grass—
   he blooms like a flower of the field;
¹⁶ when the wind passes over it, it vanishes,
   and its place is no longer known.
¹⁷ But from eternity to eternity
   the LORD's faithful love is toward those who fear him,
   and his righteousness toward the grandchildren
¹⁸ of those who keep his covenant,
   who remember to observe his precepts.
¹⁹ The LORD has established his throne in heaven,
   and his kingdom rules over all.

²⁰ Bless the LORD,
   all his angels of great strength,
   who do his word,
   obedient to his command.
²¹ Bless the LORD, all his armies,
   his servants who do his will.
²² Bless the LORD, all his works
   in all the places where he rules.
   My soul, bless the LORD!

PSALM 104
God the Creator

¹ My soul, bless the LORD!
  LORD my God, you are very great;
  you are clothed with majesty and splendor.
² He wraps himself in light as if it were a robe,
  spreading out the sky like a canopy,
³ laying the beams of his palace
  on the waters above,
  making the clouds his chariot,
  walking on the wings of the wind,
⁴ and making the winds his messengers,
  flames of fire his servants.

⁵ He established the earth on its foundations;
  it will never be shaken.
⁶ You covered it with the deep
  as if it were a garment;
  the water stood above the mountains.
⁷ At your rebuke the water fled;
  at the sound of your thunder they hurried away—
⁸ mountains rose and valleys sank—
  to the place you established for them.

What a variety of things God has made! What aspect of his creation do you especially appreciate today?

⁹ You set a boundary they cannot cross;
    they will never cover the earth again.

¹⁰ He causes the springs to gush into the valleys;
    they flow between the mountains.
¹¹ They supply water for every wild beast;
    the wild donkeys quench their thirst.
¹² The birds of the sky live beside the springs;
    they make their voices heard among the foliage.
¹³ He waters the mountains from his palace;
    the earth is satisfied by the fruit of your labor.

¹⁴ He causes grass to grow for the livestock
    and provides crops for man to cultivate,
    producing food from the earth,
¹⁵ wine that makes human hearts glad—
    making his face shine with oil—
    and bread that sustains human hearts.

¹⁶ The trees of the LORD flourish,
    the cedars of Lebanon that he planted.
¹⁷ There the birds make their nests;
    storks make their homes in the pine trees.
¹⁸ The high mountains are for the wild goats;
    the cliffs are a refuge for hyraxes.

¹⁹ He made the moon to mark the festivals;
    the sun knows when to set.
²⁰ You bring darkness, and it becomes night,
    when all the forest animals stir.
²¹ The young lions roar for their prey
    and seek their food from God.
²² The sun rises; they go back
    and lie down in their dens.
²³ Man goes out to his work
    and to his labor until evening.

²⁴ How countless are your works, LORD!
    In wisdom you have made them all;
    the earth is full of your creatures.
²⁵ Here is the sea, vast and wide,
    teeming with creatures beyond number—
    living things both large and small.
²⁶ There the ships move about,
    and Leviathan, which you formed to play there.

²⁷ All of them wait for you
    to give them their food at the right time.
²⁸ When you give it to them,
    they gather it;
    when you open your hand,
    they are satisfied with good things.

²⁹ When you hide your face,
they are terrified;
when you take away their breath,
they die and return to the dust.
³⁰ When you send your breath,
they are created,
and you renew the surface of the ground.

³¹ May the glory of the LORD endure forever;
may the LORD rejoice in his works.
³² He looks at the earth, and it trembles;
he touches the mountains,
and they pour out smoke.
³³ I will sing to the LORD all my life;
I will sing praise to my God while I live.
³⁴ May my meditation be pleasing to him;
I will rejoice in the LORD.
³⁵ May sinners vanish from the earth
and wicked people be no more.
My soul, bless the LORD!
Hallelujah!

PSALM 105
God's Faithfulness to his People

¹ Give thanks to the LORD, call on his name;
proclaim his deeds among the peoples.
² Sing to him, sing praise to him;
tell about all his wondrous works!
³ Honor his holy name;
let the hearts of those who seek the LORD rejoice.
⁴ Seek the LORD and his strength;
seek his face always.
⁵ Remember the wondrous works he has done,
his wonders, and the judgments he has pronounced,
⁶ you offspring of Abraham his servant,
Jacob's descendants—his chosen ones.

⁷ He is the LORD our God;
his judgments govern the whole earth.
⁸ He remembers his covenant forever,
the promise he ordained
for a thousand generations—
⁹ the covenant he made with Abraham,
swore to Isaac,
¹⁰ and confirmed to Jacob as a decree
and to Israel as a permanent covenant:
¹¹ "I will give the land of Canaan to you
as your inherited portion."

What looks like a setback is often a setup for God's ultimate plan to provide for his people. Ask God for eyes to see through your disappointments and temporary setbacks.

¹² When they were few in number,
   very few indeed,
   and resident aliens in Canaan,
¹³ wandering from nation to nation
   and from one kingdom to another,
¹⁴ he allowed no one to oppress them;
   he rebuked kings on their behalf:
¹⁵ "Do not touch my anointed ones,
   or harm my prophets."

¹⁶ He called down famine against the land
   and destroyed the entire food supply.
¹⁷ He had sent a man ahead of them—
   Joseph, who was sold as a slave.
¹⁸ They hurt his feet with shackles;
   his neck was put in an iron collar.
¹⁹ Until the time his prediction came true,
   the word of the LORD tested him.
²⁰ The king sent for him and released him;
   the ruler of peoples set him free.
²¹ He made him master of his household,
   ruler over all his possessions—
²² binding his officials at will
   and instructing his elders.

²³ Then Israel went to Egypt;
   Jacob lived as an alien in the land of Ham.
²⁴ The LORD made his people very fruitful;
   he made them more numerous than their foes,
²⁵ whose hearts he turned to hate his people
   and to deal deceptively with his servants.
²⁶ He sent Moses his servant,
   and Aaron, whom he had chosen.
²⁷ They performed his miraculous signs among them,
   and wonders in the land of Ham.
²⁸ He sent darkness, and it became dark—
   for did they not defy his commands?
²⁹ He turned their water into blood
   and caused their fish to die.
³⁰ Their land was overrun with frogs,
   even in their royal chambers.
³¹ He spoke, and insects came—
   gnats throughout their country.
³² He gave them hail for rain,
   and lightning throughout their land.
³³ He struck their vines and fig trees
   and shattered the trees of their territory.
³⁴ He spoke, and locusts came—
   young locusts without number.
³⁵ They devoured all the vegetation in their land
   and consumed the produce of their land.

³⁶ He struck all the firstborn in their land,
all their first progeny.
³⁷ Then he brought Israel out with silver and gold,
and no one among his tribes stumbled.
³⁸ Egypt was glad when they left,
for the dread of Israel had fallen on them.
³⁹ He spread a cloud as a covering
and gave a fire to light up the night.
⁴⁰ They asked, and he brought quail
and satisfied them with bread from heaven.
⁴¹ He opened a rock, and water gushed out;
it flowed like a stream in the desert.
⁴² For he remembered his holy promise
to Abraham his servant.
⁴³ He brought his people out with rejoicing,
his chosen ones with shouts of joy.
⁴⁴ He gave them the lands of the nations,
and they inherited
what other peoples had worked for.

⁴⁵ All this happened
so that they might keep his statutes
and obey his instructions.
Hallelujah!

PSALM 106
Israel's Unfaithfulness to God

¹ Hallelujah!
Give thanks to the LORD, for he is good;
his faithful love endures forever.
² Who can declare the LORD's mighty acts
or proclaim all the praise due him?
³ How happy are those who uphold justice,
who practice righteousness at all times.

⁴ Remember me, LORD,
when you show favor to your people.
Come to me with your salvation
⁵ so that I may enjoy the prosperity
of your chosen ones,
rejoice in the joy of your nation,
and boast about your heritage.

⁶ Both we and our fathers have sinned;
we have done wrong and have acted wickedly.
⁷ Our fathers in Egypt did not grasp
the significance of your wondrous works
or remember your many acts of faithful love;
instead, they rebelled by the sea—the Red Sea.

How quickly we forget the wonders God has done! Do some remembering today.

8 Yet he saved them for his name's sake,
  to make his power known.
9 He rebuked the Red Sea, and it dried up;
  he led them through the depths as through a desert.
10 He saved them from the power of the adversary;
  he redeemed them from the power of the enemy.
11 Water covered their foes;
  not one of them remained.
12 Then they believed his promises
  and sang his praise.

13 They soon forgot his works
  and would not wait for his counsel.
14 They were seized with craving in the wilderness
  and tested God in the desert.
15 He gave them what they asked for,
  but sent a wasting disease among them.

16 In the camp they were envious of Moses
  and of Aaron, the LORD's holy one.
17 The earth opened up and swallowed Dathan;
  it covered the assembly of Abiram.
18 Fire blazed throughout their assembly;
  flames consumed the wicked.

19 At Horeb they made a calf
  and worshiped the cast metal image.
20 They exchanged their glory
  for the image of a grass-eating ox.
21 They forgot God their Savior,
  who did great things in Egypt,
22 wondrous works in the land of Ham,
  awe-inspiring acts at the Red Sea.
23 So he said he would have destroyed them—
  if Moses his chosen one
  had not stood before him in the breach
  to turn his wrath away from destroying them.

24 They despised the pleasant land
  and did not believe his promise.
25 They grumbled in their tents
  and did not listen to the LORD.
26 So he raised his hand against them with an oath
  that he would make them fall in the desert
27 and would disperse their descendants
  among the nations,
  scattering them throughout the lands.

28 They aligned themselves with Baal of Peor
  and ate sacrifices offered to lifeless gods.
29 They angered the LORD with their deeds,
  and a plague broke out against them.

30 But Phinehas stood up and intervened,
and the plague was stopped.
31 It was credited to him as righteousness
throughout all generations to come.

32 They angered the LORD at the Waters of Meribah,
and Moses suffered because of them;
33 for they embittered his spirit,
and he spoke rashly with his lips.

34 They did not destroy the peoples
as the LORD had commanded them
35 but mingled with the nations
and adopted their ways.
36 They served their idols,
which became a snare to them.
37 They sacrificed their sons and daughters to demons.
38 They shed innocent blood—
the blood of their sons and daughters
whom they sacrificed to the idols of Canaan;
so the land became polluted with blood.
39 They defiled themselves by their actions
and prostituted themselves by their deeds.

40 Therefore the LORD's anger burned against his people,
and he abhorred his own inheritance.
41 He handed them over to the nations;
those who hated them ruled over them.
42 Their enemies oppressed them,
and they were subdued under their power.
43 He rescued them many times,
but they continued to rebel deliberately
and were beaten down by their iniquity.

44 When he heard their cry,
he took note of their distress,
45 remembered his covenant with them,
and relented according to the abundance
of his faithful love.
46 He caused them to be pitied
before all their captors.

47 Save us, LORD our God,
and gather us from the nations,
so that we may give thanks to your holy name
and rejoice in your praise.

48 Blessed be the LORD God of Israel,
from everlasting to everlasting.
Let all the people say, "Amen!"
Hallelujah!

PSALM 107
Thanksgiving for God's Deliverance

1 Give thanks to the LORD, for he is good;
his faithful love endures forever.
2 Let the redeemed of the LORD proclaim
that he has redeemed them from the power of the foe
3 and has gathered them from the lands—
from the east and the west,
from the north and the south.

4 Some wandered in the desolate wilderness,
finding no way to a city where they could live.
5 They were hungry and thirsty;
their spirits failed within them.
6 Then they cried out to the LORD in their trouble;
he rescued them from their distress.
7 He led them by the right path
to go to a city where they could live.
8 Let them give thanks to the LORD
for his faithful love
and his wondrous works for all humanity.
9 For he has satisfied the thirsty
and filled the hungry with good things.

10 Others sat in darkness and gloom—
prisoners in cruel chains—
11 because they rebelled against God's commands
and despised the counsel of the Most High.
12 He broke their spirits with hard labor;
they stumbled, and there was no one to help.
13 Then they cried out to the LORD in their trouble;
he saved them from their distress.
14 He brought them out of darkness and gloom
and broke their chains apart.
15 Let them give thanks to the LORD
for his faithful love
and his wondrous works for all humanity.
16 For he has broken down the bronze gates
and cut through the iron bars.

17 Fools suffered affliction
because of their rebellious ways and their iniquities.
18 They loathed all food
and came near the gates of death.
19 Then they cried out to the LORD in their trouble;
he saved them from their distress.
20 He sent his word and healed them;
he rescued them from the Pit.
21 Let them give thanks to the LORD
for his faithful love
and his wondrous works for all humanity.

Has the Lord redeemed you? What do you have now that you did not have before?

²² Let them offer sacrifices of thanksgiving
and announce his works with shouts of joy.

²³ Others went to sea in ships,
conducting trade on the vast water.
²⁴ They saw the LORD's works,
his wondrous works in the deep.
²⁵ He spoke and raised a stormy wind
that stirred up the waves of the sea.
²⁶ Rising up to the sky, sinking down to the depths,
their courage melting away in anguish,
²⁷ they reeled and staggered like a drunkard,
and all their skill was useless.
²⁸ Then they cried out to the LORD in their trouble,
and he brought them out of their distress.
²⁹ He stilled the storm to a whisper,
and the waves of the sea were hushed.
³⁰ They rejoiced when the waves grew quiet.
Then he guided them to the harbor they longed for.
³¹ Let them give thanks to the LORD
for his faithful love
and his wondrous works for all humanity.
³² Let them exalt him in the assembly of the people
and praise him in the council of the elders.

³³ He turns rivers into desert,
springs into thirsty ground,
³⁴ and fruitful land into salty wasteland,
because of the wickedness of its inhabitants.
³⁵ He turns a desert into a pool,
dry land into springs.
³⁶ He causes the hungry to settle there,
and they establish a city where they can live.
³⁷ They sow fields and plant vineyards
that yield a fruitful harvest.
³⁸ He blesses them, and they multiply greatly;
he does not let their livestock decrease.

³⁹ When they are diminished and are humbled
by cruel oppression and sorrow,
⁴⁰ he pours contempt on nobles
and makes them wander in a trackless wasteland.
⁴¹ But he lifts the needy out of their suffering
and makes their families multiply like flocks.
⁴² The upright see it and rejoice,
and all injustice shuts its mouth.

⁴³ Let whoever is wise pay attention to these things
and consider the LORD's acts of faithful love.

PSALM 108
A Plea for Victory
A song. A psalm of David.

1 My heart is confident, God;
I will sing; I will sing praises
with the whole of my being.
2 Wake up, harp and lyre!
I will wake up the dawn.
3 I will praise you, LORD, among the peoples;
I will sing praises to you among the nations.
4 For your faithful love is higher than the heavens,
and your faithfulness reaches to the clouds.
5 God, be exalted above the heavens,
and let your glory be over the whole earth.
6 Save with your right hand and answer me
so that those you love may be rescued.

7 God has spoken in his sanctuary:
"I will celebrate!
I will divide up Shechem.
I will apportion the Valley of Succoth.
8 Gilead is mine, Manasseh is mine,
and Ephraim is my helmet;
Judah is my scepter.
9 Moab is my washbasin;
I throw my sandal on Edom.
I shout in triumph over Philistia."
10 Who will bring me to the fortified city?
Who will lead me to Edom?
11 God, haven't you rejected us?
God, you do not march out with our armies.
12 Give us aid against the foe,
for human help is worthless.
13 With God we will perform valiantly;
he will trample our foes.

PSALM 109
Prayer against an Enemy
For the choir director. A psalm of David.

1 God of my praise, do not be silent.

2 For wicked and deceitful mouths open against me;
they speak against me with lying tongues.
3 They surround me with hateful words
and attack me without cause.
4 In return for my love they accuse me,
but I continue to pray.
5 They repay me evil for good,
and hatred for my love.

God can do in a moment what we cannot do in a lifetime. Ask for God's favor, power, and intervention today.

⁶ Set a wicked person over him;
  let an accuser stand at his right hand.
⁷ When he is judged, let him be found guilty,
  and let his prayer be counted as sin.
⁸ Let his days be few;
  let another take over his position.
⁹ Let his children be fatherless
  and his wife a widow.
¹⁰ Let his children wander as beggars,
  searching for food far from their demolished homes.
¹¹ Let a creditor seize all he has;
  let strangers plunder what he has worked for.
¹² Let no one show him kindness,
  and let no one be gracious to his fatherless children.
¹³ Let the line of his descendants be cut off;
  let their name be blotted out in the next generation.
¹⁴ Let the iniquity of his fathers
  be remembered before the LORD,
  and do not let his mother's sin be blotted out.
¹⁵ Let their sins always remain before the LORD,
  and let him remove all memory of them from the earth.

¹⁶ For he did not think to show kindness,
  but pursued the suffering, needy, and brokenhearted
  in order to put them to death.
¹⁷ He loved cursing—let it fall on him;
  he took no delight in blessing—let it be far from him.
¹⁸ He wore cursing like his coat—
  let it enter his body like water
  and go into his bones like oil.
¹⁹ Let it be like a robe he wraps around himself,
  like a belt he always wears.
²⁰ Let this be the LORD's payment to my accusers,
  to those who speak evil against me.

²¹ But you, LORD, my Lord,
  deal kindly with me for your name's sake;
  because your faithful love is good, rescue me.
²² For I am suffering and needy;
  my heart is wounded within me.
²³ I fade away like a lengthening shadow;
  I am shaken off like a locust.
²⁴ My knees are weak from fasting,
  and my body is emaciated.
²⁵ I have become an object of ridicule to my accusers;
  when they see me, they shake their heads in scorn.

²⁶ Help me, LORD my God;
  save me according to your faithful love
²⁷ so they may know that this is your hand
  and that you, LORD, have done it.

God defends and delivers those whose hearts are set on him. Entrust your story to him. And thank him by faith. It will be good for your soul.

²⁸ Though they curse, you will bless.
When they rise up, they will be put to shame,
but your servant will rejoice.
²⁹ My accusers will be clothed with disgrace;
they will wear their shame like a cloak.
³⁰ I will fervently thank the LORD with my mouth;
I will praise him in the presence of many.
³¹ For he stands at the right hand of the needy
to save him from those who would condemn him.

PSALM 110
The Priestly King
A psalm of David.

¹ This is the declaration of the LORD
to my Lord:
"Sit at my right hand
until I make your enemies your footstool."
² The LORD will extend your mighty scepter from Zion.
Rule over your surrounding enemies.
³ Your people will volunteer
on your day of battle.
In holy splendor, from the womb of the dawn,
the dew of your youth belongs to you.
⁴ The LORD has sworn an oath and will not take it back:
"You are a priest forever
according to the pattern of Melchizedek."

⁵ The Lord is at your right hand;
he will crush kings on the day of his anger.
⁶ He will judge the nations, heaping up corpses;
he will crush leaders over the entire world.
⁷ He will drink from the brook by the road;
therefore, he will lift up his head.

PSALM 111
Praise for the Lord's Works

¹ Hallelujah!
I will praise the LORD with all my heart
in the assembly of the upright and in the congregation.

² The LORD's works are great,
studied by all who delight in them.
³ All that he does is splendid and majestic;
his righteousness endures forever.
⁴ He has caused his wondrous works to be remembered.
The LORD is gracious and compassionate.
⁵ He has provided food for those who fear him;
he remembers his covenant forever.

Jesus will one day fully destroy the wicked. He will rule and reign over his people. Acknowledge him as King today.

Everything God does reveals his glory and majesty. Lean in, engage your soul, and thank him with your *whole* heart.

⁶ He has shown his people the power of his works
by giving them the inheritance of the nations.
⁷ The works of his hands are truth and justice;
all his instructions are trustworthy.
⁸ They are established forever and ever,
enacted in truth and in uprightness.
⁹ He has sent redemption to his people.
He has ordained his covenant forever.
His name is holy and awe-inspiring.

¹⁰ The fear of the LORD is the beginning of wisdom;
all who follow his instructions have good insight.
His praise endures forever.

PSALM 112
The Traits of the Righteous

¹ Hallelujah!
Happy is the person who fears the LORD,
taking great delight in his commands.

² His descendants will be powerful in the land;
the generation of the upright will be blessed.
³ Wealth and riches are in his house,
and his righteousness endures forever.
⁴ Light shines in the darkness for the upright.
He is gracious, compassionate, and righteous.
⁵ Good will come to the one who lends generously
and conducts his business fairly.
⁶ He will never be shaken.
The righteous one will be remembered forever.
⁷ He will not fear bad news;
his heart is confident, trusting in the LORD.
⁸ His heart is assured; he will not fear.
In the end he will look in triumph on his foes.
⁹ He distributes freely to the poor;
his righteousness endures forever.
His horn will be exalted in honor.

¹⁰ The wicked one will see it and be angry;
he will gnash his teeth in despair.
The desire of the wicked leads to ruin.

PSALM 113
Praise to the Merciful God

¹ Hallelujah!
Give praise, servants of the LORD;
praise the name of the LORD.
² Let the name of the LORD be blessed
both now and forever.

Want to walk in a greater measure of power? Honor God with great reverence and wonder. Pause and remember who he is today.

_____
_____
_____
_____
_____
_____

God Most High stoops down to lift us up. What has he lifted you out of? How has he raised your perspective?

_____
_____
_____
_____
_____
_____
_____

³ From the rising of the sun to its setting,
let the name of the LORD be praised.

⁴ The LORD is exalted above all the nations,
his glory above the heavens.
⁵ Who is like the LORD our God—
the one enthroned on high,
⁶ who stoops down to look
on the heavens and the earth?
⁷ He raises the poor from the dust
and lifts the needy from the trash heap
⁸ in order to seat them with nobles—
with the nobles of his people.
⁹ He gives the childless woman a household,
making her the joyful mother of children.
Hallelujah!

PSALM 114
God's Deliverance of Israel

¹ When Israel came out of Egypt—
the house of Jacob from a people
who spoke a foreign language—
² Judah became his sanctuary,
Israel, his dominion.
³ The sea looked and fled;
the Jordan turned back.
⁴ The mountains skipped like rams,
the hills, like lambs.
⁵ Why was it, sea, that you fled?
Jordan, that you turned back?
⁶ Mountains, that you skipped like rams?
Hills, like lambs?

⁷ Tremble, earth, at the presence of the Lord,
at the presence of the God of Jacob,
⁸ who turned the rock into a pool,
the flint into a spring.

PSALM 115
Glory to God Alone

¹ Not to us, LORD, not to us,
but to your name give glory
because of your faithful love, because of your truth.
² Why should the nations say,
"Where is their God?"
³ Our God is in heaven
and does whatever he pleases.

⁴ Their idols are silver and gold,
made by human hands.

The earth trembles in the presence of almighty God. May you pause and respond to his presence today.

The Lord who made heaven and earth has set his affection upon you! How are you blessed?

⁵ They have mouths but cannot speak,
eyes, but cannot see.
⁶ They have ears but cannot hear,
noses, but cannot smell.
⁷ They have hands but cannot feel,
feet, but cannot walk.
They cannot make a sound with their throats.
⁸ Those who make them are just like them,
as are all who trust in them.

⁹ Israel, trust in the LORD!
He is their help and shield.
¹⁰ House of Aaron, trust in the LORD!
He is their help and shield.
¹¹ You who fear the LORD, trust in the LORD!
He is their help and shield.
¹² The LORD remembers us and will bless us.
He will bless the house of Israel;
he will bless the house of Aaron;
¹³ he will bless those who fear the LORD—
small and great alike.
¹⁴ May the LORD add to your numbers,
both yours and your children's.
¹⁵ May you be blessed by the LORD,
the Maker of heaven and earth.
¹⁶ The heavens are the LORD's,
but the earth he has given to the human race.
¹⁷ It is not the dead who praise the LORD,
nor any of those descending into the silence of death.
¹⁸ But we will bless the LORD,
both now and forever.
Hallelujah!

PSALM 116
Thanks to God for Deliverance

¹ I love the LORD because he has heard
my appeal for mercy.
² Because he has turned his ear to me,
I will call out to him as long as I live.

³ The ropes of death were wrapped around me,
and the torments of Sheol overcame me;
I encountered trouble and sorrow.
⁴ Then I called on the name of the LORD:
"LORD, save me!"

⁵ The LORD is gracious and righteous;
our God is compassionate.
⁶ The LORD guards the inexperienced;
I was helpless, and he saved me.

When you pray, God bends down and listens. Pray with your whole heart today.

⁷ Return to your rest, my soul,
for the LORD has been good to you.
⁸ For you, LORD, rescued me from death,
my eyes from tears,
my feet from stumbling.
⁹ I will walk before the LORD
in the land of the living.
¹⁰ I believed, even when I said,
"I am severely oppressed."
¹¹ In my alarm I said,
"Everyone is a liar."

¹² How can I repay the LORD
for all the good he has done for me?
¹³ I will take the cup of salvation
and call on the name of the LORD.
¹⁴ I will fulfill my vows to the LORD
in the presence of all his people.
¹⁵ The death of his faithful ones
is valuable in the LORD's sight.
¹⁶ LORD, I am indeed your servant;
I am your servant, the son of your female servant.
You have loosened my bonds.

¹⁷ I will offer you a sacrifice of thanksgiving
and call on the name of the LORD.
¹⁸ I will fulfill my vows to the LORD
in the presence of all his people,
¹⁹ in the courts of the LORD's house—
within you, Jerusalem.
Hallelujah!

PSALM 117
Universal Call to Praise

¹ Praise the LORD, all nations!
Glorify him, all peoples!
² For his faithful love to us is great;
the LORD's faithfulness endures forever.
Hallelujah!

Pause and ponder the depths of God's love. How do you suppose he feels about you?

PSALM 118
Thanksgiving for Victory

1 Give thanks to the LORD, for he is good;
his faithful love endures forever.
2 Let Israel say,
"His faithful love endures forever."
3 Let the house of Aaron say,
"His faithful love endures forever."
4 Let those who fear the LORD say,
"His faithful love endures forever."

5 I called to the LORD in distress;
the LORD answered me
and put me in a spacious place.
6 The LORD is for me; I will not be afraid.
What can a mere mortal do to me?
7 The LORD is my helper,
Therefore, I will look in triumph on those who hate me.

8 It is better to take refuge in the LORD
than to trust in humanity.
9 It is better to take refuge in the LORD
than to trust in nobles.

10 All the nations surrounded me;
in the name of the LORD I destroyed them.
11 They surrounded me, yes, they surrounded me;
in the name of the LORD I destroyed them.
12 They surrounded me like bees;
they were extinguished like a fire among thorns;
in the name of the LORD I destroyed them.
13 They pushed me hard to make me fall,
but the LORD helped me.
14 The LORD is my strength and my song;
he has become my salvation.

15 There are shouts of joy and victory
in the tents of the righteous:
"The LORD's right hand performs valiantly!
16 The LORD's right hand is raised.
The LORD's right hand performs valiantly! "
17 I will not die, but I will live
and proclaim what the LORD has done.
18 The LORD disciplined me severely
but did not give me over to death.

19 Open the gates of righteousness for me;
I will enter through them
and give thanks to the LORD.
20 This is the LORD's gate;
the righteous will enter through it.

Storms will come and foes will oppose. But God is our Deliverer and Defender. Declare him so today.

²¹ I will give thanks to you
because you have answered me
and have become my salvation.
²² The stone that the builders rejected
has become the cornerstone.
²³ This came from the LORD;
it is wondrous in our sight.
²⁴ This is the day the LORD has made;
let us rejoice and be glad in it.

²⁵ LORD, save us!
LORD, please grant us success!
²⁶ He who comes in the name
of the LORD is blessed.
From the house of the LORD we bless you.
²⁷ The LORD is God and has given us light.
Bind the festival sacrifice with cords
to the horns of the altar.
²⁸ You are my God, and I will give you thanks.
You are my God; I will exalt you.
²⁹ Give thanks to the LORD, for he is good;
his faithful love endures forever.

PSALM 119
Delight in God's Word

א Alef

¹ How happy are those whose way is blameless,
who walk according to the LORD's instruction!
² Happy are those who keep his decrees
and seek him with all their heart.
³ They do nothing wrong;
they walk in his ways.
⁴ You have commanded that your precepts
be diligently kept.
⁵ If only my ways were committed
to keeping your statutes!
⁶ Then I would not be ashamed
when I think about all your commands.
⁷ I will praise you with an upright heart
when I learn your righteous judgments.
⁸ I will keep your statutes;
never abandon me.

ב Bet

⁹ How can a young man keep his way pure?
By keeping your word.
¹⁰ I have sought you with all my heart;
don't let me wander from your commands.
¹¹ I have treasured your word in my heart
so that I may not sin against you.

Oh, that our actions would consistently reflect God's decrees! How is the Lord calling you higher?

¹² LORD, may you be blessed;
   teach me your statutes.
¹³ With my lips I proclaim
   all the judgments from your mouth.
¹⁴ I rejoice in the way revealed by your decrees
   as much as in all riches.
¹⁵ I will meditate on your precepts
   and think about your ways.
¹⁶ I will delight in your statutes;
   I will not forget your word.

ג Gimel

¹⁷ Deal generously with your servant
   so that I might live;
   then I will keep your word.
¹⁸ Open my eyes so that I may contemplate
   wondrous things from your instruction.
¹⁹ I am a resident alien on earth;
   do not hide your commands from me.
²⁰ I am continually overcome
   with longing for your judgments.
²¹ You rebuke the arrogant,
   the ones under a curse,
   who wander from your commands.
²² Take insult and contempt away from me,
   for I have kept your decrees.
²³ Though princes sit together speaking against me,
   your servant will think about your statutes;
²⁴ your decrees are my delight
   and my counselors.

ד Dalet

²⁵ My life is down in the dust;
   give me life through your word.
²⁶ I told you about my life,
   and you answered me;
   teach me your statutes.
²⁷ Help me understand
   the meaning of your precepts
   so that I can meditate on your wonders.
²⁸ I am weary from grief;
   strengthen me through your word.
²⁹ Keep me from the way of deceit
   and graciously give me your instruction.
³⁰ I have chosen the way of truth;
   I have set your ordinances before me.
³¹ I cling to your decrees;
   LORD, do not put me to shame.
³² I pursue the way of your commands,
   for you broaden my understanding.

ה *He*

33 Teach me, LORD, the meaning of your statutes,
and I will always keep them.
34 Help me understand your instruction,
and I will obey it
and follow it with all my heart.
35 Help me stay on the path of your commands,
for I take pleasure in it.
36 Turn my heart to your decrees
and not to dishonest profit.
37 Turn my eyes
from looking at what is worthless;
give me life in your ways.
38 Confirm what you said to your servant,
for it produces reverence for you.
39 Turn away the disgrace I dread;
indeed, your judgments are good.
40 How I long for your precepts!
Give me life through your righteousness.

ו *Vav*

41 Let your faithful love come to me, LORD,
your salvation, as you promised.
42 Then I can answer the one who taunts me,
for I trust in your word.
43 Never take the word of truth from my mouth,
for I hope in your judgments.
44 I will always obey your instruction,
forever and ever.
45 I will walk freely in an open place
because I study your precepts.
46 I will speak of your decrees before kings
and not be ashamed.
47 I delight in your commands,
which I love.
48 I will lift up my hands to your commands,
which I love,
and will meditate on your statutes.

ז *Zayin*

49 Remember your word to your servant;
you have given me hope through it.
50 This is my comfort in my affliction:
Your promise has given me life.
51 The arrogant constantly ridicule me,
but I do not turn away from your instruction.
52 LORD, I remember your judgments from long ago
and find comfort.
53 Rage seizes me because of the wicked
who reject your instruction.
54 Your statutes are the theme of my song
during my earthly life.

⁵⁵ LORD, I remember your name in the night,
and I obey your instruction.
⁵⁶ This is my practice:
I obey your precepts.

ח Khet

⁵⁷ The LORD is my portion;
I have promised to keep your words.
⁵⁸ I have sought your favor with all my heart;
be gracious to me according to your promise.
⁵⁹ I thought about my ways
and turned my steps back to your decrees.
⁶⁰ I hurried, not hesitating
to keep your commands.
⁶¹ Though the ropes of the wicked
were wrapped around me,
I did not forget your instruction.
⁶² I rise at midnight to thank you
for your righteous judgments.
⁶³ I am a friend to all who fear you,
to those who keep your precepts.
⁶⁴ LORD, the earth is filled with your faithful love;
teach me your statutes.

ט Tet

⁶⁵ LORD, you have treated your servant well,
just as you promised.
⁶⁶ Teach me good judgment and discernment,
for I rely on your commands.
⁶⁷ Before I was afflicted I went astray,
but now I keep your word.
⁶⁸ You are good, and you do what is good;
teach me your statutes.
⁶⁹ The arrogant have smeared me with lies,
but I obey your precepts with all my heart.
⁷⁰ Their hearts are hard and insensitive,
but I delight in your instruction.
⁷¹ It was good for me to be afflicted
so that I could learn your statutes.
⁷² Instruction from your lips is better for me
than thousands of gold and silver pieces.

י Yod

⁷³ Your hands made me and formed me;
give me understanding
so that I can learn your commands.
⁷⁴ Those who fear you will see me and rejoice,
for I put my hope in your word.
⁷⁵ I know, LORD, that your judgments are just
and that you have afflicted me fairly.
⁷⁶ May your faithful love comfort me
as you promised your servant.

⁷⁷ May your compassion come to me
so that I may live,
for your instruction is my delight.
⁷⁸ Let the arrogant be put to shame
for slandering me with lies;
I will meditate on your precepts.
⁷⁹ Let those who fear you,
those who know your decrees, turn to me.
⁸⁰ May my heart be blameless regarding your statutes
so that I will not be put to shame.

כ *Kaf*

⁸¹ I long for your salvation;
I put my hope in your word.
⁸² My eyes grow weary
looking for what you have promised;
I ask, "When will you comfort me?"
⁸³ Though I have become like a wineskin dried by smoke,
I do not forget your statutes.
⁸⁴ How many days must your servant wait?
When will you execute judgment on my persecutors?
⁸⁵ The arrogant have dug pits for me;
they violate your instruction.
⁸⁶ All your commands are true;
people persecute me with lies—help me!
⁸⁷ They almost ended my life on earth,
but I did not abandon your precepts.
⁸⁸ Give me life in accordance with your faithful love,
and I will obey the decree you have spoken.

ל *Lamed*

⁸⁹ LORD, your word is forever;
it is firmly fixed in heaven.
⁹⁰ Your faithfulness is for all generations;
you established the earth, and it stands firm.
⁹¹ Your judgments stand firm today,
for all things are your servants.
⁹² If your instruction had not been my delight,
I would have died in my affliction.
⁹³ I will never forget your precepts,
for you have given me life through them.
⁹⁴ I am yours; save me,
for I have studied your precepts.
⁹⁵ The wicked hope to destroy me,
but I contemplate your decrees.
⁹⁶ I have seen a limit to all perfection,
but your command is without limit.

מ *Mem*

⁹⁷ How I love your instruction!
It is my meditation all day long.
⁹⁸ Your commands make me wiser than my enemies,
for they are always with me.

⁹⁹ I have more insight than all my teachers
   because your decrees are my meditation.
¹⁰⁰ I understand more than the elders
   because I obey your precepts.
¹⁰¹ I have kept my feet from every evil path
   to follow your word.
¹⁰² I have not turned from your judgments,
   for you yourself have instructed me.
¹⁰³ How sweet your word is to my taste—
   sweeter than honey in my mouth.
¹⁰⁴ I gain understanding from your precepts;
   therefore I hate every false way.

נ Nun

¹⁰⁵ Your word is a lamp for my feet
   and a light on my path.
¹⁰⁶ I have solemnly sworn
   to keep your righteous judgments.
¹⁰⁷ I am severely afflicted;
   LORD, give me life according to your word.
¹⁰⁸ LORD, please accept my freewill offerings of praise,
   and teach me your judgments.
¹⁰⁹ My life is constantly in danger,
   yet I do not forget your instruction.
¹¹⁰ The wicked have set a trap for me,
   but I have not wandered from your precepts.
¹¹¹ I have your decrees as a heritage forever;
   indeed, they are the joy of my heart.
¹¹² I am resolved to obey your statutes
   to the very end.

ס Samek

¹¹³ I hate those who are double-minded,
   but I love your instruction.
¹¹⁴ You are my shelter and my shield;
   I put my hope in your word.
¹¹⁵ Depart from me, you evil ones,
   so that I may obey my God's commands.
¹¹⁶ Sustain me as you promised, and I will live;
   do not let me be ashamed of my hope.
¹¹⁷ Sustain me so that I can be safe
   and always be concerned about your statutes.
¹¹⁸ You reject all who stray from your statutes,
   for their deceit is a lie.
¹¹⁹ You remove all the wicked on earth
   as if they were dross from metal;
   therefore, I love your decrees.
¹²⁰ I tremble in awe of you;
   I fear your judgments.

ע Ayin

¹²¹ I have done what is just and right;
   do not leave me to my oppressors.

¹²² Guarantee your servant's well-being;
do not let the arrogant oppress me.
¹²³ My eyes grow weary looking for your salvation
and for your righteous promise.
¹²⁴ Deal with your servant based on your faithful love;
teach me your statutes.
¹²⁵ I am your servant; give me understanding
so that I may know your decrees.
¹²⁶ It is time for the LORD to act,
for they have violated your instruction.
¹²⁷ Since I love your commands
more than gold, even the purest gold,
¹²⁸ I carefully follow all your precepts
and hate every false way.

פ Pe

¹²⁹ Your decrees are wondrous;
therefore I obey them.
¹³⁰ The revelation of your words brings light
and gives understanding to the inexperienced.
¹³¹ I open my mouth and pant
because I long for your commands.
¹³² Turn to me and be gracious to me,
as is your practice toward those who love your name.
¹³³ Make my steps steady through your promise;
don't let any sin dominate me.
¹³⁴ Redeem me from human oppression,
and I will keep your precepts.
¹³⁵ Make your face shine on your servant,
and teach me your statutes.
¹³⁶ My eyes pour out streams of tears
because people do not follow your instruction.

צ Tsade

¹³⁷ You are righteous, LORD,
and your judgments are just.
¹³⁸ The decrees you issue are righteous
and altogether trustworthy.
¹³⁹ My anger overwhelms me
because my foes forget your words.
¹⁴⁰ Your word is completely pure,
and your servant loves it.
¹⁴¹ I am insignificant and despised,
but I do not forget your precepts.
¹⁴² Your righteousness is an everlasting righteousness,
and your instruction is true.
¹⁴³ Trouble and distress have overtaken me,
but your commands are my delight.
¹⁴⁴ Your decrees are righteous forever.
Give me understanding, and I will live.

ק Qof

¹⁴⁵ I call with all my heart; answer me, LORD.
   I will obey your statutes.
¹⁴⁶ I call to you; save me,
   and I will keep your decrees.
¹⁴⁷ I rise before dawn and cry out for help;
   I put my hope in your word.
¹⁴⁸ I am awake through each watch of the night
   to meditate on your promise.
¹⁴⁹ In keeping with your faithful love, hear my voice.
   LORD, give me life in keeping with your justice.
¹⁵⁰ Those who pursue evil plans come near;
   they are far from your instruction.
¹⁵¹ You are near, LORD,
   and all your commands are true.
¹⁵² Long ago I learned from your decrees
   that you have established them forever.

ר Resh

¹⁵³ Consider my affliction and rescue me,
   for I have not forgotten your instruction.
¹⁵⁴ Champion my cause and redeem me;
   give me life as you promised.
¹⁵⁵ Salvation is far from the wicked
   because they do not study your statutes.
¹⁵⁶ Your compassions are many, LORD;
   give me life according to your judgments.
¹⁵⁷ My persecutors and foes are many.
   I have not turned from your decrees.
¹⁵⁸ I have seen the disloyal and feel disgust
   because they do not keep your word.
¹⁵⁹ Consider how I love your precepts;
   LORD, give me life according to your faithful love.
¹⁶⁰ The entirety of your word is truth,
   each of your righteous judgments endures forever.

שׂ Sin / שׁ Shin

¹⁶¹ Princes have persecuted me without cause,
   but my heart fears only your word.
¹⁶² I rejoice over your promise
   like one who finds vast treasure.
¹⁶³ I hate and abhor falsehood,
   but I love your instruction.
¹⁶⁴ I praise you seven times a day
   for your righteous judgments.
¹⁶⁵ Abundant peace belongs to those
   who love your instruction;
   nothing makes them stumble.
¹⁶⁶ LORD, I hope for your salvation
   and carry out your commands.
¹⁶⁷ I obey your decrees
   and love them greatly.

¹⁶⁸ I obey your precepts and decrees,
 for all my ways are before you.

ת Tav

¹⁶⁹ Let my cry reach you, LORD;
 give me understanding according to your word.
¹⁷⁰ Let my plea reach you;
 rescue me according to your promise.
¹⁷¹ My lips pour out praise,
 for you teach me your statutes.
¹⁷² My tongue sings about your promise,
 for all your commands are righteous.
¹⁷³ May your hand be ready to help me,
 for I have chosen your precepts.
¹⁷⁴ I long for your salvation, LORD,
 and your instruction is my delight.
¹⁷⁵ Let me live, and I will praise you;
 may your judgments help me.
¹⁷⁶ I wander like a lost sheep;
 seek your servant,
 for I do not forget your commands.

PSALM 120
A Cry for Truth and Peace
A song of ascents.

¹ In my distress I called to the LORD,
 and he answered me.
² "LORD, rescue me from lying lips
 and a deceitful tongue."

³ What will he give you,
 and what will he do to you,
 you deceitful tongue?
⁴ A warrior's sharp arrows
 with burning charcoal!

⁵ What misery that I have stayed in Meshech,
 that I have lived among the tents of Kedar!
⁶ I have dwelt too long
 with those who hate peace.
⁷ I am for peace; but when I speak,
 they are for war.

PSALM 121
The Lord Our Protector
A song of ascents.

¹ I lift my eyes toward the mountains.
 Where will my help come from?
² My help comes from the LORD,
 the Maker of heaven and earth.

Take your troubles to the Lord. Cry out to him, believing he will indeed answer you.

The Lord watches over your coming and your going. What questions do you have for him today?

³ He will not allow your foot to slip;
　your Protector will not slumber.
⁴ Indeed, the Protector of Israel
　does not slumber or sleep.

⁵ The LORD protects you;
　the LORD is a shelter right by your side.
⁶ The sun will not strike you by day
　or the moon by night.

⁷ The LORD will protect you from all harm;
　he will protect your life.
⁸ The LORD will protect your coming and going
　both now and forever.

PSALM 122
A Prayer for Jerusalem
A song of ascents. Of David.

¹ I rejoiced with those who said to me,
　"Let us go to the house of the LORD."
² Our feet were standing
　within your gates, Jerusalem—

³ Jerusalem, built as a city should be,
　solidly united,
⁴ where the tribes, the LORD's tribes, go up
　to give thanks to the name of the LORD.
　(This is an ordinance for Israel.)
⁵ There, thrones for judgment are placed,
　thrones of the house of David.

⁶ Pray for the well-being of Jerusalem:
　"May those who love you be secure;
⁷ may there be peace within your walls,
　security within your fortresses."
⁸ Because of my brothers and friends,
　I will say, "May peace be in you."
⁹ Because of the house of the LORD our God,
　I will pursue your prosperity.

PSALM 123
Looking for God's Favor
A song of ascents.

¹ I lift my eyes to you,
　the one enthroned in heaven.
² Like a servant's eyes on his master's hand,
　like a servant girl's eyes on her mistress's hand,
　so our eyes are on the LORD our God
　until he shows us favor.

God blesses those who bless Israel. Pray for the peace of Jerusalem. _____

Where is your gaze these days? May you lift your eyes to the Lord, stay focused on him, and do what only he tells you to do. What is the next thing he is asking you to do? _____

³ Show us favor, LORD, show us favor,
  for we've had more than enough contempt.
⁴ We've had more than enough
  scorn from the arrogant
  and contempt from the proud.

PSALM 124
The Lord Is on Our Side
A song of ascents. Of David.

¹ If the LORD had not been on our side—
  let Israel say—
² If the LORD had not been on our side
  when people attacked us,
³ then they would have swallowed us alive
  in their burning anger against us.
⁴ Then the water would have engulfed us;
  the torrent would have swept over us;
⁵ the raging water would have swept over us.

⁶ Blessed be the LORD,
  who has not let us be ripped apart by their teeth.
⁷ We have escaped like a bird from the hunter's net;
  the net is torn, and we have escaped.
⁸ Our help is in the name of the LORD,
  the Maker of heaven and earth.

PSALM 125
Israel's Stability
A song of ascents.

¹ Those who trust in the LORD are like Mount Zion.
  It cannot be shaken; it remains forever.
² The mountains surround Jerusalem
  and the LORD surrounds his people,
  both now and forever.

³ The scepter of the wicked will not remain
  over the land allotted to the righteous,
  so that the righteous will not apply their hands to injustice.
⁴ Do what is good, LORD, to the good,
  to those whose hearts are upright.
⁵ But as for those who turn aside to crooked ways,
  the LORD will banish them with the evildoers.

  Peace be with Israel.

What if the Lord had *not* been on your side? What is different about your life now that he is?

Just as the mountains surround Jerusalem, the Lord himself surrounds us with his presence and promises. Remind your soul that your strength comes from him.

PSALM 126
Zion's Restoration
A song of ascents.

1. When the LORD restored the fortunes of Zion,
   we were like those who dream.
2. Our mouths were filled with laughter then,
   and our tongues with shouts of joy.
   Then they said among the nations,
   "The LORD has done great things for them."
3. The LORD had done great things for us;
   we were joyful.

4. Restore our fortunes, LORD,
   like watercourses in the Negev.
5. Those who sow in tears
   will reap with shouts of joy.
6. Though one goes along weeping,
   carrying the bag of seed,
   he will surely come back with shouts of joy,
   carrying his sheaves.

PSALM 127
The Blessing of the Lord
A song of ascents. Of Solomon.

1. Unless the LORD builds a house,
   its builders labor over it in vain;
   unless the LORD watches over a city,
   the watchman stays alert in vain.
2. In vain you get up early and stay up late,
   working hard to have enough food—
   yes, he gives sleep to the one he loves.

3. Sons are indeed a heritage from the LORD,
   offspring, a reward.
4. Like arrows in the hand of a warrior
   are the sons born in one's youth.
5. Happy is the man who has filled his quiver with them.
   They will never be put to shame
   when they speak with their enemies at the city gate.

PSALM 128
Blessings for Those Who Fear God
A song of ascents.

1. How happy is everyone who fears the LORD,
   who walks in his ways!
2. You will surely eat
   what your hands have worked for.
   You will be happy,
   and it will go well for you.

Those who sow in tears will reap with shouts of joy. Right here in the midst of your not-yets, sow some seeds. One day you will see a harvest.

Unless the Lord protects the city, even our government officials' best efforts will fail. Seek God's mercy and protection for your city.

³ Your wife will be like a fruitful vine
   within your house,
   your children, like young olive trees
   around your table.
⁴ In this very way
   the man who fears the LORD
   will be blessed.

⁵ May the LORD bless you from Zion,
   so that you will see the prosperity of Jerusalem
   all the days of your life
⁶ and will see your children's children!

   Peace be with Israel.

PSALM 129
Protection of the Oppressed
A song of ascents.

¹ Since my youth they have often attacked me—
   let Israel say—
² Since my youth they have often attacked me,
   but they have not prevailed against me.
³ Plowmen plowed over my back;
   they made their furrows long.
⁴ The LORD is righteous;
   he has cut the ropes of the wicked.

⁵ Let all who hate Zion
   be driven back in disgrace.
⁶ Let them be like grass on the rooftops,
   which withers before it grows up
⁷ and can't even fill the hands of the reaper
   or the arms of the one who binds sheaves.
⁸ Then none who pass by will say,
   "May the LORD's blessing be on you.
   We bless you in the name of the LORD."

PSALM 130
Awaiting Redemption
A song of ascents.

¹ Out of the depths I call to you, LORD!
² Lord, listen to my voice;
   let your ears be attentive
   to my cry for help.

³ LORD, if you kept an account of iniquities,
   Lord, who could stand?
⁴ But with you there is forgiveness,
   so that you may be revered.

Though we endure many hardships on this journey, blessings and joy also belong to us because we belong to God. Make note of the fruit from your labors and the blessings from God's hand. _____

_____

_____

_____

_____

_____

We get knocked down, but we are not defeated. Jesus bore the pain and the shame for us. His victory is now our victory. Write a faith statement today.

_____

_____

_____

_____

_____

_____

⁵ I wait for the LORD; I wait
and put my hope in his word.
⁶ I wait for the Lord
more than watchmen for the morning—
more than watchmen for the morning.

⁷ Israel, put your hope in the LORD.
For there is faithful love with the LORD,
and with him is redemption in abundance.
⁸ And he will redeem Israel
from all its iniquities.

PSALM 131
A Childlike Spirit
A song of ascents. Of David.

¹ LORD, my heart is not proud;
my eyes are not haughty.
I do not get involved with things
too great or too wondrous for me.
² Instead, I have calmed and quieted my soul
like a weaned child with its mother;
my soul is like a weaned child.

³ Israel, put your hope in the LORD,
both now and forever.

PSALM 132
David and Zion Chosen
A song of ascents.

¹ LORD, remember David
and all the hardships he endured,
² and how he swore an oath to the LORD,
making a vow to the Mighty One of Jacob:
³ "I will not enter my house
or get into my bed,
⁴ I will not allow my eyes to sleep
or my eyelids to slumber
⁵ until I find a place for the LORD,
a dwelling for the Mighty One of Jacob."

⁶ We heard of the ark in Ephrathah;
we found it in the fields of Jaar.
⁷ Let us go to his dwelling place;
let us worship at his footstool.
⁸ Rise up, LORD, come to your resting place,
you and your powerful ark.
⁹ May your priests be clothed with righteousness,
and may your faithful people shout for joy.
¹⁰ For the sake of your servant David,
do not reject your anointed one.

God forgives our sins and hears our prayers. Draw nearer still. Pursue him with greater passion. Thank him for a love you can barely comprehend.

Rest and wait quietly in God's presence. You can trust him. Listen for that still, small voice today.

11 The LORD swore an oath to David,
a promise he will not abandon:
"I will set one of your offspring
on your throne.
12 If your sons keep my covenant
and my decrees that I will teach them,
their sons will also sit on your throne forever."

13 For the LORD has chosen Zion;
he has desired it for his home:
14 "This is my resting place forever;
I will make my home here
because I have desired it.
15 I will abundantly bless its food;
I will satisfy its needy with bread.
16 I will clothe its priests with salvation,
and its faithful people will shout for joy.
17 There I will make a horn grow for David;
I have prepared a lamp for my anointed one.
18 I will clothe his enemies with shame,
but the crown he wears will be glorious."

PSALM 133
Living in Harmony
A song of ascents. Of David.

1 How good and pleasant it is
when brothers live together in harmony!
2 It is like fine oil on the head,
running down on the beard,
running down Aaron's beard
onto his robes.
3 It is like the dew of Hermon
falling on the mountains of Zion.
For there the LORD has appointed the blessing—
life forevermore.

PSALM 134
Call to Evening Worship
A song of ascents.

1 Now bless the LORD,
all you servants of the LORD
who stand in the LORD's house at night!
2 Lift up your hands in the holy place
and bless the LORD!

3 May the LORD,
Maker of heaven and earth,
bless you from Zion.

King David felt compelled to finish the work God assigned to him. What about you? What assignment or calling remains unfulfilled in your life? What are your next steps? _____

God richly blesses oneness and unity, not at the expense of biblical conviction but because of it. How might God use you to build a bridge in the days ahead? _____

PSALM 135
The Lord Is Great

1 Hallelujah!
Praise the name of the LORD.
Give praise, you servants of the LORD
2 who stand in the house of the LORD,
in the courts of the house of our God.
3 Praise the LORD, for the LORD is good;
sing praise to his name, for it is delightful.
4 For the LORD has chosen Jacob for himself,
Israel as his treasured possession.
5 For I know that the LORD is great;
our Lord is greater than all gods.
6 The LORD does whatever he pleases
in heaven and on earth,
in the seas and all the depths.
7 He causes the clouds to rise from the ends of the earth.
He makes lightning for the rain
and brings the wind from his storehouses.

8 He struck down the firstborn of Egypt,
both people and animals.
9 He sent signs and wonders against you, Egypt,
against Pharaoh and all his officials.
10 He struck down many nations
and slaughtered mighty kings:
11 Sihon king of the Amorites,
Og king of Bashan,
and all the kings of Canaan.
12 He gave their land as an inheritance,
an inheritance to his people Israel.

13 LORD, your name endures forever,
your reputation, LORD,
through all generations.
14 For the LORD will vindicate his people
and have compassion on his servants.

15 The idols of the nations are of silver and gold,
made by human hands.
16 They have mouths but cannot speak,
eyes, but cannot see.
17 They have ears but cannot hear;
indeed, there is no breath in their mouths.
18 Those who make them are just like them,
as are all who trust in them.

19 House of Israel, bless the LORD!
House of Aaron, bless the LORD!
20 House of Levi, bless the LORD!
You who revere the LORD, bless the LORD!

Lift up holy hands and spend some time praising God today. Then open your hands and listen for a while. What is he asking you to do? Rest? Run? Stand? Write it down. _____

_____

_____

_____

_____

_____

Celebrities come and go, but God's fame will last forever. What idols do you see in our culture today? Declare Jesus Lord of all. _____

_____

_____

_____

_____

_____

_____

_____

²¹ Blessed be the LORD from Zion;
he dwells in Jerusalem.
Hallelujah!

PSALM 136
God's Love Is Eternal

¹ Give thanks to the LORD, for he is good.
His faithful love endures forever.
² Give thanks to the God of gods.
His faithful love endures forever.
³ Give thanks to the Lord of lords.
His faithful love endures forever.
⁴ He alone does great wonders.
His faithful love endures forever.
⁵ He made the heavens skillfully.
His faithful love endures forever.
⁶ He spread the land on the waters.
His faithful love endures forever.
⁷ He made the great lights:
His faithful love endures forever.
⁸ the sun to rule by day,
His faithful love endures forever.
⁹ the moon and stars to rule by night.
His faithful love endures forever.
¹⁰ He struck the firstborn of the Egyptians
His faithful love endures forever.
¹¹ and brought Israel out from among them
His faithful love endures forever.
¹² with a strong hand and outstretched arm.
His faithful love endures forever.
¹³ He divided the Red Sea
His faithful love endures forever.
¹⁴ and led Israel through,
His faithful love endures forever.
¹⁵ but hurled Pharaoh and his army into the Red Sea.
His faithful love endures forever.
¹⁶ He led his people in the wilderness.
His faithful love endures forever.
¹⁷ He struck down great kings
His faithful love endures forever.
¹⁸ and slaughtered famous kings—
His faithful love endures forever.
¹⁹ Sihon king of the Amorites
His faithful love endures forever.
²⁰ and Og king of Bashan—
His faithful love endures forever.
²¹ and gave their land as an inheritance,
His faithful love endures forever.
²² an inheritance to Israel his servant.
His faithful love endures forever.

Give thanks to the Lord, for his love endures *forever*. How have you seen his power manifest in your life?

²³ He remembered us in our humiliation
  His faithful love endures forever.
²⁴ and rescued us from our foes.
  His faithful love endures forever.
²⁵ He gives food to every creature.
  His faithful love endures forever.
²⁶ Give thanks to the God of heaven!
  His faithful love endures forever.

PSALM 137
Lament of the Exiles

¹ By the rivers of Babylon—
  there we sat down and wept
  when we remembered Zion.
² There we hung up our lyres
  on the poplar trees,
³ for our captors there asked us for songs,
  and our tormentors, for rejoicing:
  "Sing us one of the songs of Zion."

⁴ How can we sing the LORD's song
  on foreign soil?
⁵ If I forget you, Jerusalem,
  may my right hand forget its skill.
⁶ May my tongue stick to the roof of my mouth
  if I do not remember you,
  if I do not exalt Jerusalem as my greatest joy!

⁷ Remember, LORD, what the Edomites said
  that day at Jerusalem:
  "Destroy it! Destroy it
  down to its foundations! "
⁸ Daughter Babylon, doomed to destruction,
  happy is the one who pays you back
  what you have done to us.
⁹ Happy is he who takes your little ones
  and dashes them against the rocks.

PSALM 138
A Thankful Heart
Of David.

¹ I will give you thanks with all my heart;
  I will sing your praise before the heavenly beings.
² I will bow down toward your holy temple
  and give thanks to your name
  for your constant love and truth.
  You have exalted your name
  and your promise above everything else.
³ On the day I called, you answered me;
  you increased strength within me.

Ask God for a song in the night. Trust him to make things right. Sing to him and him alone.

⁴ All the kings on earth will give you thanks, LORD,
  when they hear what you have promised.
⁵ They will sing of the LORD's ways,
  for the LORD's glory is great.
⁶ Though the LORD is exalted,
  he takes note of the humble;
  but he knows the haughty from a distance.

⁷ If I walk into the thick of danger,
  you will preserve my life
  from the anger of my enemies.
  You will extend your hand;
  your right hand will save me.
⁸ The LORD will fulfill his purpose for me.
  LORD, your faithful love endures forever;
  do not abandon the work of your hands.

PSALM 139
The All-Knowing, Ever-Present God
For the choir director. A psalm of David.

¹ LORD, you have searched me and known me.
² You know when I sit down and when I stand up;
  you understand my thoughts from far away.
³ You observe my travels and my rest;
  you are aware of all my ways.
⁴ Before a word is on my tongue,
  you know all about it, LORD.
⁵ You have encircled me;
  you have placed your hand on me.
⁶ This wondrous knowledge is beyond me.
  It is lofty; I am unable to reach it.

⁷ Where can I go to escape your Spirit?
  Where can I flee from your presence?
⁸ If I go up to heaven, you are there;
  if I make my bed in Sheol, you are there.
⁹ If I live at the eastern horizon
  or settle at the western limits,
¹⁰ even there your hand will lead me;
  your right hand will hold on to me.
¹¹ If I say, "Surely the darkness will hide me,
  and the light around me will be night"—
¹² even the darkness is not dark to you.
  The night shines like the day;
  darkness and light are alike to you.

¹³ For it was you who created my inward parts;
  you knit me together in my mother's womb.
¹⁴ I will praise you
  because I have been remarkably and wondrously made.
  Your works are wondrous,
  and I know this very well.

God's promises are backed by the honor of his name. What promises are you holding on to today?

¹⁵ My bones were not hidden from you
when I was made in secret,
when I was formed in the depths of the earth.
¹⁶ Your eyes saw me when I was formless;
all my days were written in your book and planned
before a single one of them began.

¹⁷ God, how precious your thoughts are to me;
how vast their sum is!
¹⁸ If I counted them,
they would outnumber the grains of sand;
when I wake up, I am still with you.

¹⁹ God, if only you would kill the wicked—
you bloodthirsty men, stay away from me—
²⁰ who invoke you deceitfully.
Your enemies swear by you falsely.
²¹ LORD, don't I hate those who hate you,
and detest those who rebel against you?
²² I hate them with extreme hatred;
I consider them my enemies.
²³ Search me, God, and know my heart;
test me and know my concerns.
²⁴ See if there is any offensive way in me;
lead me in the everlasting way.

PSALM 140
Prayer for Rescue
For the choir director. A psalm of David.

¹ Rescue me, LORD, from evil men.
Keep me safe from violent men
² who plan evil in their hearts.
They stir up wars all day long.
³ They make their tongues
as sharp as a snake's bite;
viper's venom is under their lips.   *Selah*

⁴ Protect me, LORD,
from the power of the wicked.
Keep me safe from violent men
who plan to make me stumble.
⁵ The proud hide a trap with ropes for me;
they spread a net along the path
and set snares for me.   *Selah*

⁶ I say to the LORD, "You are my God."
Listen, LORD, to my cry for help.
⁷ LORD, my Lord, my strong Savior,
you shield my head on the day of battle.

Humbly open your hands and ask God to search your heart, to point out anything in you that offends him. Then wait and listen. What is the Lord saying to you?

⁸ LORD, do not grant the desires of the wicked;
do not let them achieve their goals.
Otherwise, they will become proud.   Selah

⁹ When those who surround me rise up,
may the trouble their lips cause overwhelm them.
¹⁰ Let hot coals fall on them.
Let them be thrown into the fire,
into the abyss, never again to rise.
¹¹ Do not let a slanderer stay in the land.
Let evil relentlessly hunt down a violent man.

¹² I know that the LORD upholds
the just cause of the poor,
justice for the needy.
¹³ Surely the righteous will praise your name;
the upright will live in your presence.

PSALM 141
Protection from Sin and Sinners
A psalm of David.

¹ LORD, I call on you; hurry to help me.
Listen to my voice when I call on you.
² May my prayer be set before you as incense,
the raising of my hands as the evening offering.

³ LORD, set up a guard for my mouth;
keep watch at the door of my lips.
⁴ Do not let my heart turn to any evil thing
or perform wicked acts
with men who commit sin.
Do not let me feast on their delicacies.
⁵ Let the righteous one strike me—
it is an act of faithful love;
let him rebuke me—
it is oil for my head;
let me not refuse it.
Even now my prayer is against
the evil acts of the wicked.
⁶ When their rulers will be thrown off
the sides of a cliff,
the people will listen to my words,
for they are pleasing.

⁷ As when one plows and breaks up the soil,
turning up rocks,
so our bones have been scattered
at the mouth of Sheol.

⁸ But my eyes look to you, LORD, my Lord.
I seek refuge in you; do not let me die.

In every generation and nation, there are the voiceless, the poor, the oppressed, and the slave. Who is God calling you to speak up for today?

_____

_____

_____

_____

_____

_____

_____

_____

What do you say about your life, your circumstances, your loved ones, and even your enemies? Ask the Lord to redeem your words and empower your speech.

_____

_____

_____

_____

_____

⁹ Protect me from the trap they have set for me,
  and from the snares of evildoers.
¹⁰ Let the wicked fall into their own nets,
  while I pass by safely.

PSALM 142
A Cry of Distress
A Maskil of David. When he was in the cave. A prayer.

¹ I cry aloud to the LORD;
  I plead aloud to the LORD for mercy.
² I pour out my complaint before him;
  I reveal my trouble to him.
³ Although my spirit is weak within me,
  you know my way.

  Along this path I travel
  they have hidden a trap for me.
⁴ Look to the right and see:
  no one stands up for me;
  there is no refuge for me;
  no one cares about me.

⁵ I cry to you, LORD;
  I say, "You are my shelter,
  my portion in the land of the living."
⁶ Listen to my cry,
  for I am very weak.
  Rescue me from those who pursue me,
  for they are too strong for me.
⁷ Free me from prison
  so that I can praise your name.
  The righteous will gather around me
  because you deal generously with me.

PSALM 143
A Cry for Help
A psalm of David.

¹ LORD, hear my prayer.
  In your faithfulness listen to my plea,
  and in your righteousness answer me.
² Do not bring your servant into judgment,
  for no one alive is righteous in your sight.

³ For the enemy has pursued me,
  crushing me to the ground,
  making me live in darkness
  like those long dead.
⁴ My spirit is weak within me;
  my heart is overcome with dismay.

When you are overwhelmed, all alone, or buried under your circumstances, call on the name of the Lord. He will hear your cry and save you. Call on him today.

⁵ I remember the days of old;
 I meditate on all you have done;
 I reflect on the work of your hands.
⁶ I spread out my hands to you;
 I am like parched land before you.   Selah

⁷ Answer me quickly, LORD;
 my spirit fails.
 Don't hide your face from me,
 or I will be like those
 going down to the Pit.
⁸ Let me experience
 your faithful love in the morning,
 for I trust in you.
 Reveal to me the way I should go
 because I appeal to you.
⁹ Rescue me from my enemies, LORD;
 I come to you for protection.
¹⁰ Teach me to do your will,
 for you are my God.
 May your gracious Spirit
 lead me on level ground.

¹¹ For your name's sake, LORD,
 let me live.
 In your righteousness deliver me from trouble,
¹² and in your faithful love destroy my enemies.
 Wipe out all those who attack me,
 for I am your servant.

PSALM 144
A King's Prayer
Of David.

¹ Blessed be the LORD, my rock
 who trains my hands for battle
 and my fingers for warfare.
² He is my faithful love and my fortress,
 my stronghold and my deliverer.
 He is my shield, and I take refuge in him;
 he subdues my people under me.

³ LORD, what is a human that you care for him,
 a son of man that you think of him?
⁴ A human is like a breath;
 his days are like a passing shadow.

⁵ LORD, part your heavens and come down.
 Touch the mountains, and they will smoke.
⁶ Flash your lightning and scatter the foe;
 shoot your arrows and rout them.

What in your life feels unsteady right now? May God's gracious Spirit steady your steps and lead you to a stable place.

⁷ Reach down from on high;
 rescue me from deep water, and set me free
 from the grasp of foreigners
⁸ whose mouths speak lies,
 whose right hands are deceptive.

⁹ God, I will sing a new song to you;
 I will play on a ten-stringed harp for you—
¹⁰ the one who gives victory to kings,
 who frees his servant David
 from the deadly sword.
¹¹ Set me free and rescue me
 from foreigners
 whose mouths speak lies,
 whose right hands are deceptive.

¹² Then our sons will be like plants
 nurtured in their youth,
 our daughters, like corner pillars
 that are carved in the palace style.
¹³ Our storehouses will be full,
 supplying all kinds of produce;
 our flocks will increase by thousands
 and tens of thousands in our open fields.
¹⁴ Our cattle will be well fed.
 There will be no breach in the walls,
 no going into captivity,
 and no cry of lament in our public squares.
¹⁵ Happy are the people with such blessings.
 Happy are the people whose God is the LORD.

PSALM 145
Praising God's Greatness
A hymn of David.

¹ I exalt you, my God the King,
 and bless your name forever and ever.
² I will bless you every day;
 I will praise your name forever and ever.

³ The LORD is great and is highly praised;
 his greatness is unsearchable.
⁴ One generation will declare your works to the next
 and will proclaim your mighty acts.
⁵ I will speak of your splendor and glorious majesty
 and your wondrous works.
⁶ They will proclaim the power of your awe-inspiring acts,
 and I will declare your greatness.
⁷ They will give a testimony of your great goodness
 and will joyfully sing of your righteousness.

Our trials will serve us in the end if we will be trained by them.

What battles are you facing right now? What is God teaching you amidst those trials?

⁸ The LORD is gracious and compassionate,
 slow to anger and great in faithful love.
⁹ The LORD is good to everyone;
 his compassion rests on all he has made.
¹⁰ All you have made will thank you, LORD;
 the faithful will bless you.
¹¹ They will speak of the glory of your kingdom
 and will declare your might,
¹² informing all people of your mighty acts
 and of the glorious splendor of your kingdom.
¹³ Your kingdom is an everlasting kingdom;
 your rule is for all generations.
 The LORD is faithful in all his words
 and gracious in all his actions.
¹⁴ The LORD helps all who fall;
 he raises up all who are oppressed.
¹⁵ All eyes look to you,
 and you give them their food at the proper time.
¹⁶ You open your hand
 and satisfy the desire of every living thing.
¹⁷ The LORD is righteous in all his ways
 and faithful in all his acts.
¹⁸ The LORD is near all who call out to him,
 all who call out to him with integrity.
¹⁹ He fulfills the desires of those who fear him;
 he hears their cry for help and saves them.
²⁰ The LORD guards all those who love him,
 but he destroys all the wicked.
²¹ My mouth will declare the LORD's praise;
 let every living thing
 bless his holy name forever and ever.

PSALM 146
The God of Compassion

¹ Hallelujah!
 My soul, praise the LORD.
² I will praise the LORD all my life;
 I will sing to my God as long as I live.

³ Do not trust in nobles,
 in a son of man, who cannot save.
⁴ When his breath leaves him,
 he returns to the ground;
 on that day his plans die.

⁵ Happy is the one whose help is the God of Jacob,
 whose hope is in the LORD his God,
⁶ the Maker of heaven and earth,
 the sea and everything in them.
 He remains faithful forever,

God grants the desires of those who fear him. He hears their cry and saves them. Call on the Lord, pour out your heart, and then do what he says.

⁷ executing justice for the exploited
and giving food to the hungry.
The LORD frees prisoners.
⁸ The LORD opens the eyes of the blind.
The LORD raises up those who are oppressed.
The LORD loves the righteous.
⁹ The LORD protects resident aliens
and helps the fatherless and the widow,
but he frustrates the ways of the wicked.

¹⁰ The LORD reigns forever;
Zion, your God reigns for all generations.
Hallelujah!

PSALM 147
God Restores Jerusalem

¹ Hallelujah!
How good it is to sing to our God,
for praise is pleasant and lovely.

² The LORD rebuilds Jerusalem;
he gathers Israel's exiled people.
³ He heals the brokenhearted
and bandages their wounds.
⁴ He counts the number of the stars;
he gives names to all of them.
⁵ Our Lord is great, vast in power;
his understanding is infinite.
⁶ The LORD helps the oppressed
but brings the wicked to the ground.

⁷ Sing to the LORD with thanksgiving;
play the lyre to our God,
⁸ who covers the sky with clouds,
prepares rain for the earth,
and causes grass to grow on the hills.
⁹ He provides the animals with their food,
and the young ravens, what they cry for.

¹⁰ He is not impressed by the strength of a horse;
he does not value the power of a warrior.
¹¹ The LORD values those who fear him,
those who put their hope in his faithful love.

¹² Exalt the LORD, Jerusalem;
praise your God, Zion!
¹³ For he strengthens the bars of your city gates
and blesses your children within you.
¹⁴ He endows your territory with prosperity;
he satisfies you with the finest wheat.

Do not put your confidence in powerful people. Whose opinion matters more than it should? It is God who establishes and equips you. Reset your perspective today.

God heals the brokenhearted and he puts the stars in place. He is right here and he's out there. He rules the waves and he calms your heart. Thank him for all aspects of his character today.

¹⁵ He sends his command throughout the earth;
   his word runs swiftly.
¹⁶ He spreads snow like wool;
   he scatters frost like ashes;
¹⁷ he throws his hailstones like crumbs.
   Who can withstand his cold?
¹⁸ He sends his word and melts them;
   he unleashes his winds, and the water flows.

¹⁹ He declares his word to Jacob,
   his statutes and judgments to Israel.
²⁰ He has not done this for every nation;
   they do not know his judgments.
   Hallelujah!

PSALM 148
Creation's Praise of the Lord

¹ Hallelujah!
  Praise the LORD from the heavens;
  praise him in the heights.
² Praise him, all his angels;
  praise him, all his heavenly armies.
³ Praise him, sun and moon;
  praise him, all you shining stars.
⁴ Praise him, highest heavens,
  and you waters above the heavens.
⁵ Let them praise the name of the LORD,
  for he commanded, and they were created.
⁶ He set them in position forever and ever;
  he gave an order that will never pass away.

⁷ Praise the LORD from the earth,
  all sea monsters and ocean depths,
⁸ lightning and hail, snow and cloud,
  stormy wind that executes his command,
⁹ mountains and all hills,
  fruit trees and all cedars,
¹⁰ wild animals and all cattle,
   creatures that crawl and flying birds,
¹¹ kings of the earth and all peoples,
   princes and all judges of the earth,
¹² young men as well as young women,
   old and young together.
¹³ Let them praise the name of the LORD,
   for his name alone is exalted.
   His majesty covers heaven and earth.
¹⁴ He has raised up a horn for his people,
   resulting in praise to all his faithful ones,
   to the Israelites, the people close to him.
   Hallelujah!

Thank God for things you've not thanked him for in a while (running water, butterflies, fresh watermelon, the sun, the moon and the stars, and so on).

PSALM 149
Praise for God's Triumph

1 Hallelujah!
Sing to the LORD a new song,
his praise in the assembly of the faithful.
2 Let Israel celebrate its Maker;
let the children of Zion rejoice in their King.
3 Let them praise his name with dancing
and make music to him with tambourine and lyre.
4 For the LORD takes pleasure in his people;
he adorns the humble with salvation.
5 Let the faithful celebrate in triumphal glory;
let them shout for joy on their beds.

6 Let the exaltation of God be in their mouths
and a double-edged sword in their hands,
7 inflicting vengeance on the nations
and punishment on the peoples,
8 binding their kings with chains
and their dignitaries with iron shackles,
9 carrying out the judgment decreed against them.
This honor is for all his faithful people.
Hallelujah!

PSALM 150
Praise the Lord

1 Hallelujah!
Praise God in his sanctuary.
Praise him in his mighty expanse.
2 Praise him for his powerful acts;
praise him for his abundant greatness.

3 Praise him with trumpet blast;
praise him with harp and lyre.
4 Praise him with tambourine and dance;
praise him with strings and flute.
5 Praise him with resounding cymbals;
praise him with clashing cymbals.

6 Let everything that breathes praise the Lord.
Hallelujah!

Warfare and worship go hand in hand. Take a moment to thank God for his mighty power, then pray about some of the concerns on *his* heart.

There is no one like our God. Tell him so!